This book will change your life! For those that d̤̈ ̤̈ou will start to understand the schemes of the Devil (the ̤̈ ̤̈cking you coming into His Glorious Light.

It's such a privilege to have ̤̈ ̤̈e has opened not only my eyes, bṳ̈ ̤̈to a deeper revelation of God's love and goṳ̈ ̤̈y, I could not put the book down.

If you need answers in your life ̤̈ ̤̈re struggling to defeat sickness, abuse and oppression, then Nicole's b̤̤̈̈antly honest and raw testimony will pave the way to your freedom.

Yes, we are in a battle on this planet Earth, but God has given us all the keys and the authority to be over-comers! We don't need to live in defeat anymore.

I'm blown away at the changes in Nicole in just over two years. She has been healed from lung cancer, abuse, sickness, depression, oppression, guilt and shame and she is now riding with the armies of Heaven beside her, dressed in white and declaring, "Yes Lord we will Ride".

Frances 'Fran' Bridges

God and Horses

Finding God at 42

A TESTIMONY OF BEING DELIVERED FROM
DEPRESSION AND OVERCOMING CANCER.

NICOLE BORTOLUSSI
WITH THE HOLY SPIRIT

Ark House Press
arkhousepress.com

© 2024 Nicole Bortolussi

All rights reserved. Apart from any fair dealing for the purpose of study, research, criticism, or review, as permitted under the Copyright Act, no part may be reproduced by any process without written permission.

Scriptures marked NKJ® are taken from the New King James Version®. Copyright © 1982 by Thomas Nelson. Used by permission. All rights reserved.

Scriptures marked ESV® are taken from The ESV® Bible (The Holy Bible, English Standard Version®), © 2001 by Crossway, a publishing ministry of Good News Publishers. Used by permission. All rights reserved.

Scriptures marked NIV® are taken from the Holy Bible, New International Version®, NIV®. Copyright © 1973, 1978, 1984, 2011 by Biblica, Inc.™ Used by permission of Zondervan. All rights reserved worldwide. www.zondervan.com The "NIV" and "New International Version" are trademarks registered in the United States Patent and Trademark Office by Biblica, Inc.™

Scriptures marked NASB® are taken from the New American Standard Bible®, Copyright © 1960, 1971, 1977, 1995, 2020 by The Lockman Foundation. Used by permission. All rights reserved. lockman.org "

Some names and identifying details have been changed to protect the privacy of individuals.

Cataloguing in Publication Data:
Title: God and Horses
ISBN: 978-1-7637394-9-9 (pbk)
Subjects: REL012170   RELIGION / Christian Living / Personal Memoirs; PET006000   PETS / Horses; REL012040   RELIGION / Christian Living / Inspirational;

Design by initiateagency.com

Find me on Facebook:
God and horses by Nicole Bortolussi

Dedication

I dedicate this book to the Lord my God, my saviour, my love, my redeemer. Thank you for being the greatest, most forgiving Father, all glory is Yours.

Thank you Jesus for the transformation of my mind, body, soul and for saving me eternally.

Thank you Holy Spirit for practically writing this book for me, and leading me to all truth, the greatest friend I have ever known.

Thank you to all the amazing humans, whom I can now call family.

God bless you all ... Enjoy!

Contents

Chapter 1	Do you ever get that feeling…	1
Chapter 2	Horses and me	17
Chapter 3	Poisoning myself and finding God	27
Chapter 4	Flood visions. Proof of God	41
Chapter 5	Delivered from depression, the beginning of wisdom	48
Chapter 6	Fellowship begins	67
Chapter 7	2023 Tragic revelations	76
Chapter 8	The one word you never want to hear. Cancer	86
Chapter 9	Teeth and cigarettes	106
Chapter 10	Merroo. A 20-year wait.	117
Chapter 11	Dreamer of dreams.	130
Chapter 12	A whole new person	153

Chapter 1

DO YOU EVER GET THAT FEELING...

Do you ever get that feeling that there's much more to the world. More than what we are told. More than we are taught.

School just teaches us about the physical, what we can see, hear, touch, smell, taste. About history, geography, math, english, sports, but nothing about what we can sense, feel, experience, certainly nothing about anything supernatural. Not that I remember anyway! Yes, there was religion, but that was never presented as a supernatural answer, more as a way to remove freedom than to give it. Dark and sombre, many religions involving appeasing their gods of wrath. Not bringing answers or a guide to living well.

Since a child I always sensed there was something more, something bigger, something supernatural. It took me 42 years to figure out what that was, so that everything made sense, so the puzzle pieces all came together, and blessedly I did get there. I did find out the truth, and the truth turned out to be better and more amazing, more fulfilling than I ever could have imagined. The truth more surprisingly brought relief, peace and joy, something very unexpected. The truth lifted a weight I never knew I carried, a hand over of worry, a lifting of depression and anxiety, of mental torment, a disbelief of my own ignorance that makes me still laugh, a truth so simple that had been there all along: God.

Growing up I had pretty much what I would call an average middle-class family, but in hindsight we all think that we have the average normal family. Mine was Mum, Dad, one 18-month younger brother, grandparents that lived around the corner, and others that lived overseas in New Zealand. Spending Christmas and Easter at a family lunch, the occasional holiday at the beach that we drove to and the less occasional visit to family in New Zealand. Going to catholic schools in both primary and secondary, then off to university. I did what I thought was expected of me, what the world said was the thing to do, following a path many others had followed before me.

We sat as a family and had dinner every night. We talked about our day, about school, and that was that. I can look back now and tell you we weren't close, we weren't friends, we never talked about feelings or the future. Advice was never given about life or how to live it, we never talked about how to make good choices or be good people. Nor about how to treat others or how we should be treated. We never talked about the world, or politics, or religion, or what we wanted to do in the future. Dad would have called himself Catholic and Mum Christian, though I never knew this about Mum. God was definitely never spoken about, never brought up. We did not go to church unless it was Christmas or Easter and even that stopped when I was still a small child. We were never part of a church community, the Bible was never read, nor did I see anyone reading it. We never told each other we loved each other or cared about each other. My parents rarely hugged or kissed each other, and never us children. My parents fought a lot, big fights, tears, screaming, hate, anger. We ate our food together at the table each night and went our separate ways.

I had a lot of freedom, as long as I kept out of the way and did not get into any trouble. I did actually get up to a lot of trouble but was never caught so they never knew. They did not ever ask if I was OK or about how I was feeling or even if I did my schoolwork. I did not even know these were questions that parents asked. I just remember fighting endless fighting. I thought this was a normal household, how everybody grew up. My friends thought I had it great, I was allowed to do as I pleased. In reality, I was very lost and stumbling and crashing my way through life, making bad choices with no guidance, trusting the wrong people as I went. My greatest asset and biggest struggle was my mind. I was bright and did not struggle to learn, but anxiety and depression would grab me, get a hold of me, trap me, it escalated in my teens. My mind and emotions would swirl and struggle, dip and dive, I was desperate for escape. I beat myself up mentally. I had no one to turn to, so when it all got too much, I would drop everything and run away from life. I never understood what was wrong with me. I always felt very misunderstood and alone. Tormented. I was looking for something I just did not know what.

The idea of God was laughable, inconceivable, if you had asked me in my teens, 20s, 30s I would have told you the Bible was a book written by four stoned guys Mathew, Mark, Luke, and John. They wrote a bestseller. Religion class in school was a time to chat with friends and make fun of the Nuns. Any sort of church service meant hiding in the toilets, then ducking out the front gate to enjoy some free time when our absence was not noticed.

A religious school meant that it was all girls, the boys went to a different school. It meant teachers seemed to care more about our dresses being neat and tidy, than anything to do with our relationship or belief in God. Nothing to do with how to live our lives, or how to have a relationship with God, or what that meant, maybe they did not know themselves.

Horses had always been an animal I loved and had a passion for since a child. Being incredibly lucky to get my first horse at 13, after a series of unfortunate events. My parents never intended to buy me a horse, neither could they afford it, but end up with a horse I did, much to my own amazement. It truly made me happy. I saw my horse once a week, I would spend hours riding in the bush and made a new friend, the love of horses creating a friendship that's now lasted over 30 years.

My horse was an escape from real life. I was amazed at the level of communication and trust that was able to be achieved with this huge half a ton creature that was so gentle and tried so hard. Horses were so forgiving and so kind. They were an animal I could pour my empathy into, that would never betray me or let me down. Horses lived in the moment. When I was with my horse I was at peace, my mind was consumed, I wasn't thinking, I was just being. It felt more like how the world was supposed to be.

As I grew older, I went to university and started working. I started to believe in more the idea of karma, which seemed to make sense where religion hadn't. The idea of your own actions coming back around. Which gave some guidance to how to make choices and why things were the way they were. An understanding of why good or bad things happened. That we could somehow have control, influence how things would be. If we were good, good things would follow. How false this would prove to be.

New age beliefs of horoscopes and tarot cards also came into play, I found these fascinating and wondered of the validity of such things. Could we know the future? And if we knew the future could we avoid disaster, find happiness. This was still the early 2000s so scrolling and randomly finding new ideas, new ways of thinking hadn't really come into anyone's lives just yet. It was still an era of meeting people, being told stories and doing research. Buying books. Being given books. Going to the library. It's a different world we live in now, where we stumble across ideas we would never have considered. The endless scrolling. Back then the supernatural just brought forward ideas of ghosts, horror movies, witches, magic, the x-files and aliens. God and the Bible had nothing to do with anything supernatural as far as I was concerned.

Then everything changed, when in 2000 I had a bad car accident. I remember it like it was yesterday. It was my final year of university. I had been having car trouble, when I put my foot on the clutch the engine of the car cut out, not every time, nor every gear change. Though it seemed to be happening more often as my journey progressed, it was very distracting, I kept having to restart the car, but as long as I was moving, I could clutch start it. The problem was if I came to a halt, I needed to use the key, it was easier if the car was still rolling and I could use the clutch start. Finally, I'd made it to the final turn into the university gates, a set of traffic lights, a right turn where I needed to cross 3 lanes of traffic doing 80km / hr. The lights were green, but the right turn arrow wasn't green, I didn't notice. The car ahead of me went, without thinking I followed.

I didn't see it coming. I heard it, the sound of metal on metal, glass shattering, the force of the impact throwing my body around. I can only describe what happened next as my mind splitting in 2, from the shock, the realisation of what was happening. I have 2 memories of this moment. The first memory which lives in reality where the whole accident lasts 3 seconds if that, the 8 tonne truck ploughing into the front of the passenger side, my car spinning, my body being thrown to the side, the seat belt grabbing me, the huge noise, metal crunching, glass exploding, everything stopping as quickly as it started. I was extremely blessed that day, walking away with only a small cut on my face, and a broken collar bone from being thrown forward and into the side of the car. My car was destroyed, the police officer telling my father he was amazed I walked away that day.

Then there is the second memory, where time slowed down, the one sound a single high tone, white if sound was a colour, zero fear, complete clarity, time stretching, pausing almost, the single line of thought that came to me and in that moment was completely true. That right at the moment I could die, that this could be the end, and then the complete peace which came over me. It seemed to last minutes, then zoom I was back, sitting in the car which had now stopped, realising what had happened, that I was still alive. The pain in my shoulder, the faces appearing at the window telling me not to move, help was coming, reality.

Even today, more than 20 years later, that moment in time, those two memories, are as clear as if they had happened yesterday. That feeling of time slowing down, would come back to me many other times over the course of my life. I was starting to understand more and more that there was more. Nothing I could quite grasp, nothing I could yet understand, nothing that made sense. 20 more years would pass before I would finally find the truth.

Another couple of years passed, I was now in my early 20s, my childhood best friend, the one I'd made friends with through horses, started having what I could only call supernatural experiences. She would meet a person, and all of a sudden start telling them all about their past and people they had lost. Images rattling through her head, she was never wrong, this happened multiple times with multiple strangers. I was amazed, fascinated and somewhat envious. She would tell strange stories of things she was seeing, but after this went on for about 6 months, she got increasingly scared and overwhelmed, trying to understand what was happening in her head. There was no one to ask, so little information available, she ended up going to a Buddhist temple, they helped her to turn it off, to block the images coming into her mind.

This led her into the new age beliefs as a way to try and understand what had happened. Why and how she had seen what wasn't there, she was never able to tap into it again as she had over that time, the Buddhists had successfully blocked it. She discovered tarot reading and it became an obsession, multiple decks, so many books. She would spend thousands of hours over the following years, talking to people doing research. Trying to get a look into the future and trying to understand what she had seen. Why she has seen it, even taking up tarot reading herself as a career. Which she has continued to do for over 20 years. Again, I was fascinated and loved to play around with the idea of knowing the future, but it was all so hit and miss, more like gambling than any sort of guide to life or something to put any faith into.

I tried to live a life that was more expected of me which involved university, work, travel but it all felt so pointless. I was always so restless. I would finally get settled in study or work, then depression would creep up on me again, I would drop everything and run away, trying to find an escape from that heavy weight. Each time I started something new it would lift, but only for a time, then depression would slowly creep back upon me, take over again, a vicious cycle of trying to find peace of mind, which was always so fleeting.

There was something else in me, that has always been a part of my life that I never understood, that never made sense, a weird second sense of the world, of the future, that we would call "the knowing". Where big events would happen, big shocking changes, and I would have a sense of "knowing" an image in my head long beforehand, a memory of an event that had not happened yet. Where that feeling from the car accident, where time had almost slowed down, would return as the "knowing" became a real-life event. As I grew older, I could describe these "knowings" much more clearly, they would come to pass, usually years later, but never in ways I thought they would occur. I would also come to learn they were a marker of a momentous change. The mark of an event that would turn my life upside down, they would come to me with years between the mental image (the knowing) and the real life event. So, they were never something I put much trust into, only the occasional wonder of what it meant, or a discussion of when I thought it might happen. I was always wrong! I'd say over the years there's been maybe a dozen of these "knowings". I didn't realise when I was younger how important they were, hindsight at its best.

The first "knowing" came to me as a teen, though I never told anyone, I had this weird thought that I would receive an inheritance early, but in my logical brain that meant that both my parents would have to pass early, a scary thought, a car or plane crash perhaps, when a local kid killed both his parents in order to get access to their finances, that freaked me right out. Surely, I'd never do that, but this idea sat with me for years. How or why would I receive an early inheritance, sadly this "knowing" came to be correct. The first one. I remember the day I was told my father was dieing, it was a slow-mo moment in time like the car accident, as my brain tried to comprehend that reality and the "knowing" had become one and the same. Like recalling a memory rather than being told something new. When my father passed three weeks later, his estate was split between myself, my brother and mother, rather than all going directly to my mother. An unusual set of circumstances. I had received my inheritance early. I didn't quite know what to make of it. How I already knew, it was a very strange feeling, made no sense in the reality I lived in, at the time I told nobody, for fear of sounding nuts.

The next "knowing" occurred with a friend of my partners twin girls, there was something about twins that felt so familiar, like I already knew, but you question yourself, think you are silly, irrational, then during the same time in 2006 during my father's short time from diagnosis to death,

DO YOU EVER GET THAT FEELING...

I found out I was pregnant, with twins! I remember the day clearly, going for an ultrasound to confirm my pregnancy, the technician at first telling me I had polyps then the pause, oh wait, actually you are having twins. It was again like I slow-mo moment in time, zero shock, I already knew, it was a lot to take in. I couldn't comprehend how this was happening, what it meant, how I knew.

It was a couple of years later before I had another "knowing" form in my head. I can't quite explain the moment it happens. How they form, maybe they come in dreams I forget. It's like having a memory of something you had forgotten, except the knowing isn't something you are remembering from times passed, it's something that you are remembering that hasn't happened yet. The next "knowing" was a memory of a phone call, a significant phone call, it would be dark and the cordless phone next to my bed would wake me. The person on the other end would tell me something that would come as a huge shock. It was over 5 years between the forming of the knowing and the real event. I hadn't learnt yet it wouldn't be a good shock, I had hoped it would be the lotto office calling to tell me I had won! Instead, it was a call being told the man I was in love with, whom I totally trusted, had been lying through his teeth, that I had been totally deceived. I was devastated and heartbroken, shocked to my core, it didn't seem real. Again, another huge life event, a disaster, my mental health plummeted.

There are other "knowings" I will recall as my story goes on, even now sitting down to write this, to finally tell my story is something that seems so familiar, something I always knew I would do. Write. I thought I'd write a story about all the horses I had trained, the people I had met. There are some crazy stories, but nope! This is a story I never could have ever guessed I would live, a typical "knowing", completely catching me off guard. I can never understand until I'm living it. God was never on my radar. But he had plans.

With hindsight I definitely think "the knowing " is something that has been passed down from my father, a generational thing. There were quite a few times when I was in my teens, and into my 20's, that he had told me he only had 10 years to live, that he would die young. Which very much tied in with my own "knowing" and concern about my parents dieing, but I never took him too seriously as nothing yet had come to pass. I didn't know the "knowing" was a *knowing*. I also never realised until after his death, that I was the only one he had told that he wasn't going to live to be an old man, that he would die young, that he only had 10 years. His "knowing" perhaps, when he did find out he was sick, stage 4 cancer, he fully accepted it and embraced it, passing less than 4 weeks later. He was ready to go, he had been expecting it, he even had a farewell party to say goodbye to all of his friends. It's a shame really, that it was only because of his death did my own first "knowing" come true. I'll always wonder if, like me, he had many "knowings" throughout his life, what his stories were, I'll never know.

I had always felt a bit lost in life, if anybody had asked me what I wanted to be when I grew up, I would have drawn a complete blank. I really didn't have a clue. I had no real plans or dreams for the future. I didn't dream about a certain job, getting married or having kids like other people did. My future wasn't something I was ever asked about by my parents, or ever discussed at home, there was definitely no "knowing" in this regard. I guess I always hoped there was some bigger picture, that there was a reason and explanation for life, some guide for what I was supposed to do with the future.

After university before getting pregnant and before Dad died, I had stumbled around trying to figure out life. Working different jobs, studying more and travelling, trying to find my way, not really knowing what was next or what the future held. I had no real goals, nobody ever asked where

I saw myself. There was never really any plan and the future felt like a big black hole. I was trying to survive my own mind.

By the time my father did pass, I was 26 years old and pregnant with twins (a boy and a girl) to a man I'd only been dating for just over a year. He was nearly 20 years older than me and parenthood was not something I was prepared for, I had no idea what I was getting myself into. I was just living to survive as life turned into a nightmare with this man. He was abusive and I experienced a terrible season of domestic violence. I finally escaped just before the twins' second birthday, moving some 500 kms away, to hide from the terror that had become my reality.

But it was not to be. We returned home to Sydney 12 months later after the house burnt down! Yes, you read that right. 10am one morning a fire started and the house burnt to the ground. We had nowhere to go, so we returned to Sydney to live with Mum for a couple of months. As strange as my life goes, it worked out for the best. Things had settled down and we were no longer getting threats or being intimidated. The children's father had moved on with another woman, and we were safe. Again, I hoped there was something more to life, but being a single parent of twins was all consuming, so I didn't think about it too much. When I did think about it, all I could come up with was that nothing I did really mattered. I was just a speck of life, of dust, of matter, an accident cause by a big explosion, occurring at this time in history by chance, and by the time my children's children were adults I would be much forgotten. Like my own grandparents would mean nothing to my children, just old photos on the wall, my day-to-day life, my feelings especially, would mean nothing to anybody else but me. Even my children at this young age would forget most things. I just needed to survive, especially survive my own head which I was always battling with. Depression and anxiety were a constant in my life, the friends I wished would leave.

Though this way of thinking, as to nothing mattered, didn't fit with the "knowing" nor did the idea of the supernatural, that really did seem to exist. Perhaps what we did, the decisions we made did matter in the grand scheme of things, maybe not religion, but something else, something bigger than me.

As the years passed, more and more experiences were building up that really didn't fit into the whole idea of life as simply what we just could see, hear, smell and touch, especially as other things had occurred where there was no denying it, one of those being when I saw the ghosts!

It was during an incident after my children were born, while I was still with their father. All my senses were on high alert, like a prey animal being hunted. He was angry, drunk and unpredictable. I had run to hide in my bedroom on the top level (3 stories up, because we lived in a flood zone). Every sense was blazing trying to hear where in the house he was, trying to be one step ahead. I was terrified not knowing how badly things would escalate, wondering if I should again call the police. The number of the local station written in permanent marker on the plastic phone base. It was much quicker to call directly than call 000 as I didn't have to explain. They had been here many times before. Going to a window to see if I could see him out there, I looked down to the lawn. Instead, I saw something that still seems unbelievable. An aboriginal man dressed as he would have been over 200 years before hand, an animal skin as a loin cloth and designs painted on his skin dancing up and down the lawn. A huge "wait, what," moment! Time stood still. It was night and he circled around in the light cast from the house and moonlight. I backed away from the window shocked, after a few moments time looked again to see if I had just imagined what I saw. But nope there he still was, dancing to music I couldn't hear. I retreated again; the fear caused by the children's father was forgotten. Finally, after one more retreat and return to again look out the window he was gone, vanished.

I don't remember what happened the rest of that night, whether it was a night I called the police or not, nor how far things escalated. I don't remember if I got hurt or anything was broken. But I sure do remember that ghost dancing up and down the lawn like it was yesterday. Further adding to my belief that there was more to the world than I understood, this was something from fantasy from movies and stories, from the *Dream Time* perhaps.

I was no less shocked when it happened again months later, same situation. The kid's Dad, drunk and angry and me on high alert. This time I saw a woman, out of a different window, the opposite side of my bedroom. I couldn't see her face, blocked by the top of the window, only her old-style clothes from a more convict era, her arms hanging by her sides and a rope around her neck, from which she had been hung, her feet dangling. I think this time I was less scared, but the distraction of something being broken in another room and me turning around, meant that when I turned back, she was gone.

Were they ghosts? Spirits? Something else? Memories from the past that crossed time? The history of the area I lived in, in the Hawkesbury, meant that both aboriginals and early white settlers would have lived here or nearby, especially considering 1km down the street is a huge lagoon, the seasonal creek that drains into it running behind my house. Australia is a place where water is scarce so no doubt people would have made use of the lagoon over thousands of years. Sadly, the history of the area also involved much conflict between white man and the aboriginals. With a massacre of the aboriginals occurring in the early 1800's. So, the idea that both the dancing man and the woman had both lived and or died here was more than a possibility.

Again, I didn't know what this all meant, nor how the world really worked, but another layer was added to my fascination that there was something more to the world. What, I had no clue, nor where to get answers from. There are so many different ideas proposed from so many different cultures, especially when the idea of life on other planets is brought into the mix. But interestingly the idea of God at this time in life seemed the most absurd, and least likely to have any sort of answers. It's quite funny really how the truth is right there in front of us and we are just too blind, ignorant and stubborn to see it, 2 billion people can't be right can they!

In the meantime, it would still be more than 10 years before I would find the truth, before God would become part of my life. My guiding light, my saviour, my sanity. Until then I was on my own, and I did a great job making bad decisions, trusting the wrong people. Unbeknownst to me, I was actually following many of the principles the Bible provided, but without any sense of discernment, or understanding of the enemy. The evil in life that would want to bring me undone. I had zero protection.

In trying to do the right thing, never to judge people, help everyone that needed help or asked for help, I brought people into my life that very much took advantage. At one stage within the same 6 months, I found myself allowing into my life 2 different compulsive liars. Both these humans caught me very much off guard. I believed everything they said. I had no concept that people could lie so much, that people could create their own reality in complete opposition to the truth. That once exposed and found out, that someone could change so much in the blink of an eye. Incidents like this really threw me, and affected my mental health in a very negative way. I just didn't understand how people could be this way, but learn I did not! I kept having this blind faith in others, so kept learning the hard way. I desperately wanted to believe that at their core people are essentially good. I didn't really believe in evil, we were after all just an accident of the universe, a big bang come to life. How could there be good and evil? Surely everyone deserves a chance. I did find good people along my journey, but they always seemed few and far between. I seemed to be a magnet for trouble.

By not understanding how the world worked, and hanging onto the concept of karma, I hoped that if I kept doing the right thing then good things would come. I kept thinking I must have done something to deserve being treated this way. I desperately wanted answers I could never find.

Abusive relationships are a strange beast, from the outside I'm sure I come across as a strong independent person, someone unlikely to ever be in a relationship where I was controlled by another person. But sadly, it doesn't work that way, and for the second time in my life around 2014, I found myself with a man, whom at the drop of a hat would turn violent. It was a devastating situation. I didn't understand how I was back here again, it felt shameful, living in fear, needing to call the police for help. People say just leave but it's not that easy, not that simple, you do leave but they don't. They keep coming back, you are trying not to trigger them, you walk on eggshells, they talk you around, it becomes a horrible cycle you're desperate to escape. Unless you have lived it it's impossible to understand, sadly it's not an uncommon situation. Domestic violence, abuse, control, so many people have lived it, are living it. The abusers are often the most charming, interesting, nicest, most helpful people you will ever meet, inch by inch they take control, brainwash you, you don't realise it's happening until it's too late, you have been lured into the trap.

Then once you do escape, you are in survival mode, your brain doesn't function like normal, you are on constant high alert, distracted. You never think it will happen to you, especially for a second time. I can't explain it. I literally got trained, another couple of years would pass before I was completely free again.

In hindsight growing up, my parents had a terrible marriage. So, I never understood or saw what a good relationship looked like. Because I was in a head space of bad mental health, I was appreciative that anybody would want me, put up with me, putting very little value on myself. This just opened the door for all the wrong people. Relationships had started to become a trigger for depression itself. Since that time, although I've dated a couple of people, I've never really been in a relationship again, it's just been easier that way.

Horses and my kids became my life. I didn't know there was anything else to live for. I hoped things would get better, but instead I would be faced with many more challenges, only finally getting relief in the last 2 years when I finally found God, and a whole new me was born, when I could finally find safety and protection.

Chapter 2

HORSES AND ME

Like many young girls as a child, I loved horses. I was very lucky when at 9 years old I was allowed riding lessons at the local riding school. It was a place that was far from fancy, but as a little girl I was clueless of that! When my parents agreed to let me have lessons it was on one condition, that I understood that I was never going to have my own horse, which I understood and agreed to, heck I was only 9.

For the next 2 years I had intermittent lessons at the riding school, nothing regular, also occasionally being allowed to attend the holiday program. Pony for a day, spending the whole day for 5 full days in a row. It's almost sad to see old photos, the state of the shaggy half dead ponies I would have ridden, their long coats and sad eyes, but I was clueless to that and adored those horses. Happy to spend any time with any horse, my non horsey parents were clueless also. I certainly didn't fall into the category of the girls who rode regularly, with their fancy show ponies who attended the local pony club. I was at best a beginner and never progressed past this stage. I was about 11 when the riding school finally closed, as often happens in cities. The population grew, those few remaining paddocks being sold to developers for houses and apartments to be built. Many of those paddocks are now office towers. My riding journey came to a halt.

A couple of years passed and I was now in high school. I had made new friends, 2 of these being a set of twins whose father had bought them a horse! I was amazed and we quickly became friends through this common bond. I was invited to come visit their horse a chance I jumped at, these girls had less riding experience than even myself, having only plodded around on trail horses, so I seemed like an expert! I was thrilled to be given a chance to ride and spend time with a horse again.

The place where they kept their horse, was a huge property on the outskirts of Sydney, a trail riding business also ran from this property, so there was literally 100s of horses there, both on agistment (people paying to keep their horse there), and used by the business from which people hired horses to ride.

Then it happened, although years beforehand I was given the rule no horse, when a horse of their friend came up for sale, I was more than persistent in asking my parents if we could buy this horse, if I could have my own. The price was 800 with all the gear, saddles etc. I was told that was very cheap, and the 50 a week agistment cost seemed like nothing to my 13-year-old brain, so I begged my parents, endlessly no doubt. Dad finally agreed to letting me try this horse. I was over the moon and day dreamed this horse would be mine, not knowing at the time that he had zero intention of ever buying the horse. He just wanted to shut me up, I expect. But disaster struck!

Remember I really was clueless, and I'm sure I over estimated my abilities! So, when the day came the owner of the horse put me on board, riding another horse herself, took me out for a ride on the 600 acres property. We were miles from home when she asked me if I wanted to go faster, if I wanted to canter up the hill, of course I did, so off we went. Before I knew it my horse was totally out of control, myself overtaking her, not being able to stop. I'm not sure if the horse did anything wrong, but losing my balance and falling off is what I did do, my first fall, going at speed onto the hard red dirt. I wasn't badly injured, but I was definitely knocked around, bruised but not broken, I had gotten a bad fright. The owner caught the horse, being too scared to get back on. I led the horse, quite a few kms back home. I was devastated, all my dreams of my own horse shattered, my body hurt and walking so far on that hot day was torture.

Upon returning I broke down in tears, my heart broken, my concerned father packing me in the car and taking me home. Shocked as much as I was at the outcome of the day. But God I'm sure stepped in, or planned the whole thing. Because a couple of weeks later, we learnt of another horse for sale, this time an older mare who was actually completely suitable for 500 dollars. This time my parents actually took pity on me I'm sure, and purchased the horse, a wonderful palomino mare who taught me how to ride properly and brought endless joy. My perfect match.

So, without that fall, the horrid walk home and the heartbreak that followed, I would never have ever owned a horse in the first place! A guiding hand, I believe so! My first life lesson in resilience.

Over the next 4-5 years I had a couple of different horses, I grew out of each one, literally as I'm now 6'4, each horse was sold and a bigger horse bought. By the time I was nearly 18 and high school was coming to an end, all the exams and study meant time was becoming very limited, and it was decided my horse owning journey would need to end for now. I agreed and my horse, a huge black thoroughbred was sold, my gear packed into the cupboard, but not forgotten.

I was maybe 22 - 23 before horses became a big part of my life again, and my next big lesson would begin. Though I had stayed friends with the girl from the riding place, on the outskirts of Sydney. The same friend who also became a psychic. She had never had a break from owning a horse, owning many different horses over the years, our friendship meant that I could still spend time with horses and ride when I wanted, in the gaps where I didn't have my own.

By 21 university had finished, I then travelled around Australia and overseas. Over the next couple of years I also studied more. But I just couldn't find work I enjoyed, that kept me sane. Every job I started I would eventually run away from as my mental health would take me down a dark road, anxiety would begin, followed by its friend depression. It was still the early 2000s and mental health was still not something talked about, still very stigmatised and misunderstood, shameful even. I wasn't diagnosed, running away and isolation had become a very unhealthy coping strategy. But I just didn't understand what was going on in my own head. I just knew if I changed something, moved, travelled, started something new I would feel better, but it never lasted. Life was never boring with me around; I was far from scared of change. I thrived with constant change. The next adventure was just around the corner, but it couldn't last forever, having children stopped this cycle, but for now this was how I lived.

One day trying to figure out what to do next, I was looking through jobs and discovered a job for working at a horse-riding school about 90 mins away. I jumped at the chance. The job involved learning to be a horse-riding instructor. I didn't blink at the long drive or terrible pay. I applied and got the job. I was thrilled.

I stayed at this job for nearly 2 years. I won't write too much, but it was another lesson in resilience, about enduring. My boss was a hard woman, borderline mean, she expected myself and another girl to work our butts off, never complain and never say no. We would do huge weeks, in all-weather including weekends for what would work out to be less than $5 an hour, as it was considered training like a university or tafe course, and we would get an accreditation at the end. Which I never did, but did I learn a lot? Absolutely, she was an amazing horse woman. I would watch and soak up every bit of wisdom I could. The horses always came first and were very well looked after, even if us humans weren't! Eventually, like always my mental health broke, and it was time to move on. I just couldn't cope with such high expectations and zero thanks, being treated like that, and although I tried to find another job with horses, nobody else quite put the horses first like she did. She was terrible with the human side, but the horses never ever missed out, they thrived.

During that time, I learnt invaluable lessons. I learnt to work hard, how to push through my comfort zone, past exhaustion, I learnt how horses learnt and how to communicate with them, I learnt to do as I was told, I learnt to listen and watch to notice the small things, I learnt to keep my mouth shut and not complain, I learnt to work with an animal that couldn't talk, but always tried so hard gave their all, I learnt the horses came first. I didn't know it at the time, but God would later use all these lessons to teach me about Him. How he came first, how even in my discomfort and exhaustion to keep going, how to watch and listen for small things, how to learn how he was teaching me and communicating with me, and how to do as I was told, but unlike this horse experience, Gods lessons once I got through the hard bit and learnt the lesson, gave me endless peace and joy, huge rewards. I wouldn't need to run anymore. God would be my place of rest finally.

But I didn't know this yet, it would be many many years. Obviously, God knew I needed more lessons before His classes started! Another 6 years passed before the next big life lessons began, and I bought a horse that would change my life.

It was now around late 2010 early 2011. We had lost the house to fire and had returned to Sydney. Mum was being a great help with the kids on weekends, and they had started preschool 2 days a week. I had blocks of time to myself for the first time in years, so I started to ride my horses weekly rather than the random occasion as I had been doing.

I had 2 horses at the time, Willow a huge 16.3h thoroughbred gelding I'd owned for years, since the riding school job and Flicka a young green appaloosa mare I was enjoying training. Putting into practice everything I had learnt over the years. I had come to the conclusion that I would sell Willow, as he was now so quiet I thought he would be a blessing to another person, and find another young horse to continue to learn to train.

In looking to buy another horse, I didn't know then what I do now, people lie! Especially when selling a horse, they don't want, which has a problem that no one else will want either. So, when I came upon an advert for a 9 year old grey Arab that was "green", I jumped at the chance to own this beautiful horse. The woman on the phone seemed very nice and honest. I didn't realise her telling me she has others looking at the horse, and her creating a sense of urgency was a red flag. I immediately agreed to buy the horse and arranged a day to pick him up. The horse was located 3 hours away, upon arrival she wasn't there, her partner met me, another red flag, and I was shown the sorriest and saddest looking horse I had ever seen, nothing like the photos. So very underweight, with ribs and spine showing. The pile of old vegetables on the ground I was told by the guy were his feed. Collected from out of a dumpster, by this stage I should have had alarm bells screaming in my ears, but nope, empathy took over. I didn't even try to negotiate the price. I handed him the money, caught the horse and loaded him in the float with zero drama. I suspect he was as happy to leave as I was to get him out of there!

Over the next couple of months, I just fed the poor horse and made friends with him. He turned from a bag of bones into a gorgeous grey Arab, something from a picture book, a fairy-tale horse. Then came time to ride, although the horse had been in a sorry state, I still didn't realise how badly I'd been lied to, so when my first attempt to mount this green horse ended with a rodeo, followed by me eating dirt, it started to dawn on me how many red flags I'd actually missed, lots!

Perspective is a funny thing, a lot of people would have been scared by a bucking horse, common sense would have kicked in. Me not so much, I knew real fear, I knew what it was like to have an abusive alcoholic terrorise me. This horse's actions weren't anywhere near that scary, his reaction happened in a moment and was over, this was a terrified horse. As scared as I had once been, my empathy again kicked in. I felt bad for the horse, so what did I do? I went looking for answers. I wanted to help this horse, and that's exactly what I did, was it an easy road, heck no, did I eat dirt again, yes, a few times! Did I ever give up, definitely not! Did in turn I start to find myself again, and heal from the trauma of being abused, yes. Did I find self-confidence and joy in life again, yes! 18 months passed before the horse was reliably safe to ride, looking at him you wouldn't have thought it was the same horse, he was a picture of health, the journey, the highs and lows, had brought me so much, a sense of accomplishment and joy. When I was working with this horse, I found a peace of mind I hadn't experienced before. I knew this was the direction my life needed to go in, especially when I tracked back the horse's previous history. Ignorance is bliss sometimes, the original owner, the one prior to the lady I bought him from, had sent this same horse to 4 different trainers, and spent thousands of dollars. Still the horse was unrideable, whereupon she sold him to the girl I'd purchased him from. She was very relieved when I contacted her, to find out although the horse had gotten himself into a bad situation, he had found me and there was a happy ending, she even came and visited. I was not expecting the story she told me, knowing I had been able to retrain a horse where four other trainers had failed. I knew I was doing something right!

Would I have ever bought this horse if I had known his history of failed trainers? Heck no! Did I learn a lot much about myself and my own capabilities from this horse? Absolutely. I wanted more, I wanted to help another horse. So, after much consideration I put him up for sale. Was I honest? Yes. 100%. I told people who contacted me the whole story and subsequently I sold him to an amazing new owner. Sadly, I lost contact with his new owner when I lost my phone and got a new number, but the last I had heard was his favourite drink was champagne, so I knew everything worked out for the best. He wouldn't find himself in a bad situation again, his future was secure.

At the time I still didn't know where all this was headed. I didn't know I would end up training horses professionally full time for over 10 years. I didn't know all the amazing horses I would get to work with. I didn't know how many friends I would make, or people I would meet. I didn't know how much I would learn. I also didn't know how much dirt I would eat! Though I've never gotten hurt badly, I've never needed a hospital trip, no doubt God's guiding hand caught me, more than a few times I've landed on my feet, literally! I just knew that I had a lot of fun, felt a great sense of accomplishment, and had saved this horse's life, and I wanted to do it again.

So, I bought another horse, and then another, and then another. Retrained and resold. Was I lied to again? Absolutely, more than once. I'm a sucker and way too trusting, in all aspects of life, but there were blessings, and I did find myself an amazing mentor, in John O'Leary. Someone more than trustworthy. Someone to ask questions to, someone that wouldn't mince words, someone that knew the answers when I didn't, who would call me out on mistakes without worrying if it hurt my feelings, who would tell me straight! I have so much gratitude for all his advice and guidance, coming from another state 1000's of kilometres away. God put him on my path no doubt about it, he was my 'Horse Bible', with all the answers! I just had to be willing to listen and take no offence, be humble, more lessons that would prove invaluable when God showed up in my life.

So how did I end up a professional and unexpectedly making a living out being a horse trainer. Simple. I was honest, although I was lied to about the horses when I bought them, I never lied when I sold them. I would literally tell the buyer the horse's whole life story, and spend hours chatting to potential buyers. Only wanting the right match for the horse, to secure their future. I didn't realise at the time this was unusual. I didn't realise that I was building trust and a reputation. I was just compelled to do the right thing, find the right homes for these horses which I so came to adore. To protect the horses from ever being in a situation again where they weren't looked after, to find them homes where they would be kept forever.

And so little by little people started asking me to help with another horse they had at home in the paddock, that they were having problems with, or tell their friend about me, recommend me, and so without trying or advertising a business grew. I never had long wait lists. I was never very well known, until you found yourself in trouble buying the wrong horse or sending your horse to a trainer that sent them home with issues that made them unrideable, then if you started asking around you might have come across me. I was never big or fancy. I did everything myself, training and care. I needed to know the horses inside out, to be able to gain their trust and help them overcome their fears or behaviours. Over the next 11 years I was never out of work, as soon as I'd think I needed to advertise the phone would ring and I would have more work, a new client.

Were there horses I couldn't help, yes, pain and injury are things that can trigger undesirable behaviour in horses, to help these horses, I created relationships with other trustworthy professionals I met along the way, and referred the horse to them. I always did my utmost to do the right thing by the owner, but especially by the horse.

But as time passed, I became the problem, my own health became my biggest hurdle, my body was breaking down, not knowing what was wrong was so very frustrating. As the years passed that hurdle grew bigger and bigger, until it was a mountain I could no longer cross and by 2021 I was forced to stop, my own declining health had beaten me, but I was very blessed as it was at that exact moment of defeat, of brokenness, that God entered my life.

Chapter 3

POISONING MYSELF AND FINDING GOD

Ever since I was a child, I've had gut issues and mental health difficulties. From panic attacks and depression, to endless allergies and immune system issues. It was over 30 years ago now that I did my first elimination diet at 13. Something that is now so common was unheard of back then. I remember Mum trying to figure out how to feed me dairy free and gluten free, the food that was available was extremely limited and usually horrid. I ended up living off grilled chicken and pears for what seemed like years on end. Especially when I was told I was allergic to dairy, which meant that way of eating was going to be a permanent change. "Dairy disease" one of the High school girls coined it, no one had ever heard of food allergies in the 90s. I was just blessed to have a mother with some medical knowledge, who was stubborn enough to question the doctors and request other specialists, not just go down the road it was all in my head. Sadly though there was also a lot in my head! But mental health was very much taboo, and less spoken of than food allergies in those days. The one time I did see a psychologist, they brought up Mum's own upbringing and she quickly pulled me out of there never to return, not wanting to think her own childhood or life could have any effect on me. Could it have helped, I'll never know.

Over 20 years passed, the time was around 2013, and I was now 34 years old. My twins were 6 or 7, I had just been hurt badly by being lied to by someone I loved and trusted; after surviving domestic violence by the children's father and finally letting myself fall in love again, this came as a huge blow and my mental health finally broke. Depression got hold of me so bad that I finally decided it was time to try medication on the prompting my mother and doctors. After years of saying no. Not wanting to go down that road.

It was Mum who convinced me, telling me depression runs in the family and was a chemical imbalance. Something I would have to live with forever, learn to manage my whole life. After trying an antidepressant that didn't agree with me, Zoloft, whereby I lost a lot of weight and couldn't sleep, we finally settled on paroxetine, the same medication Mum took. Aropax, its brand name, Mum had been taking for years. It seemed the sensible thing to do. Did it work, yes, I thought so, the depression didn't feel quite so bad. Did I talk to a psychologist and come up with other strategies, no. This was never suggested or advised. Not by Mum or my doctor, so I diligently took the antidepressant, every day without fail for the next 8years. If I missed a few days or a week, I felt myself start to falter, the anxiety would start to rise, and the depression start to creep back in. I became dependent, scared to not take those little white pills, they felt like sanity, not being depressed became a big focus of my life. I believed after all that I was sick. I believed I had a condition that ran in my family, that I would have to learn to manage for the rest of my life.

The kids hadn't been in school long, it was around 2014 - 2015 when the gut issues first started to come up. Nausea and bloating became a regular part of life, after speaking to the doctor, with my previous history of allergies, it made sense to be a food related issue. So back on the elimination diet I went, removal of different food groups appeared to help, even if for only a short time. Specialist appointments ruled out coeliac and any severe allergies, yet even with the most restrictive diets the issues remained. Among the different diets I tried I was even a gluten free vegan for 3 months, the most restrictive diet you will ever come across. I now understand why vegans become food obsessed. It takes so much prep and planning, it takes over hours of the day, grabbing a basic snack is even tricky. Eating out was a nightmare! Not that I ever ate out.

I even went down the whole leaky gut theory, removing lecithin, while being a gluten free vegan! But nope, nothing stopped me waking every morning coughing up bile, nor me getting sick throughout the day, sweating, cramps, and doubled over in pain. I thought my incessant cough was smoking related, but nope, later the cough disappeared, while I was still smoking, something I would never have believed at the time.

As time passed the symptoms escalated, I rarely left home, as I never knew when the cramps would start and I would need to bolt for the toilet. It was year's before I understood that what was happening was actually overheating and getting heat stroke. There was a couple of times that I in fact didn't make it home to the toilet, and as a woman in their 30s, the risk of being out and literally soiling myself just triggered more anxiety. I became very good at avoiding leaving the house, even something as simple as attending a school sports day felt impossible. My poor kids missed out on alot. As time passed the weight also slowly crept on, even though I was eating virtually nothing. I really didn't understand what was wrong with me, the lack of empathy from doctors just made it worse. As far as they were concerned, I was exaggerating. I felt like a nuisance, so slowly stopped going as much.

Then in 2019, after a friend realised how sick I was after staying with me, dragged me to a new doctor, another referral, and a gastroenterologist then decided time for cameras in both ends. I was told I had ulcers, gastritis, polyps and haemorrhoids, and was given medication to treat, but no real answers why. The medication it turned out was just a band aid, but at the time I was very glad to have some answers, to know it wasn't just in my head, but didn't realise even with medication I would continue to get worse.

Basically, I was miserable, tired and hot. Months would pass without me leaving home. At the time I didn't realise that although I was drinking 3 -4l of fluids a day, usually ice-cold cordial, my thirst was never quenched. The fact that I would be working, get hot, then all of a sudden start coughing and get sick. I never realised it was from my body temp increasing, no doctor ever suggested it. I was getting heat stroke and badly dehydrating, constantly, daily, no wonder I had ulcers. But I didn't know this at the time. I just didn't know why I felt so awful, it was very much getting me down.

My job training horses, which I loved, was getting harder and harder to do. Fatigue would kick in so quickly, and I was constantly getting sick. Breaking into a coughing fit, then running for the toilet was an endless cycle. Psoriasis which I also suffered from, now covered over half my body. I looked a mess, feeling sick and itchy was my normal, a kind of living hell I tried to hide.

I was also having terrible nightmares, so there was no escape, not even in sleep. Slowly after years of this, wine became my friend, an escape after an awful day. At least in the evening I could pretend this wasn't happening. I could sleep and not dream, my restless sleep was my only respite, yet the 12 - 14 hrs I often slept didn't stop the feeling of being tired. I struggled to wake up every morning, and would set 4 or 5 alarms, many of which I would sleep through. It was embarrassing, especially when I was being woken by a client arriving, I would then have to race to get dressed and put on a happy face. I'd jokingly say ooops to many wines last night, I forgot the alarm, rather than try and explain the misery I was trying to survive. It felt endless, I didn't know what to do but keep going. I certainly couldn't switch jobs; I was too much of a mess and there's no way anyone would have hired me! But bills need to be paid and life goes on, so keeping on going was all I could do.

The arrival of covid in 2020 in a lot of ways was a relief, then it wasn't just me, nobody was leaving their house, job keeper which the government provided to keep small business going meant I could actually scale back as everyone's lives for the next 2 years stopped and started with each lockdown. There weren't clients here daily, just the ladies whose horses lived here on agistment, and they already knew I was unwell and struggling health wise, so didn't have to explain to them.

The doctors, and yes, I went to multiple, still couldn't really tell me what was wrong. Bloods and other tests were all normal, mentally and physically I was broken, this had now been going on for years with no end in sight.

Eventually I just stopped going to doctors, I felt judged and that no one really cared. I had gotten good at hiding things from friends and family as I continued to get worse. I hated talking about it. I felt like I was imagining it, to my kids having a tired cranky sick mother was just their normal, sadly they got used to me being like that. That's who I was, we never went out for the day to do anything fun and a holiday was something other people did.

As time passed, I just tried to put on my happy mask every day, to show the world, I just got on with life. Coughing up bile every morning, struggling to keep my mental health in check, never leaving home was just what happened, I couldn't see an end to it. I'm sure people looking in from the outside thought I had some sort of drug problem, turns out little did I know they weren't wrong!

But then something did happen, my whole life was about to change, in ways that still shock me!

My phone was a distraction from real life, a way to tune out and not think too much, as I'm sure it is for many. An addiction almost, a place to hide from reality, especially during covid and all the craziness of the world. For over 2 years we lived in a world that hadn't existed before. A horror movie of sorts, where would all this craziness lead to nobody knew. The future was something we waited to unfold, to see how things would turn out, covid controlled everyone's lives.

During this time and my endless scrolling, I watched many documentaries, went down many rabbit holes. Then one day I came across a documentary about the Bible, something I would normally have flicked past, have zero interest in, but something caught my attention that day so I watched fascinated. It wasn't about the content of the Bible like I had thought of it, the ramblings of a few stoned guys, this documentary was about the Bible being a historically correct document, wait what! Not true I thought, 13 years of catholic school and I had never heard such a thing. I thought the Bible was some abstract book that had been used to scare and control people, nothing to do with actual real-life events or real people, but my interest was captured, so watch I did, enthralled with this new revelation.

Over the next few weeks I discovered, not only was the Bible accurate historically, which blew my mind, but the truth of it. I thought stories of Moses, David and Goliath, Jonah and the whale were all fairy tales, more like Disney stories. Not actual true stories, wow why didn't the nuns ever teach us this! I might have showed up to the class!

I also discovered something that captured my attention further and again blew my mind, something known as Bible prophecy, whereby every one of the more than 2000 prophecies the Bible had of the future had come true, as written, in correct order. The odds of that are beyond impossible! This was definitely never taught in catholic school! The Bible tells the future! Mind blown.

Already having experienced the "knowing" and understanding that's exactly what much of the new age stuff is attempting to achieve. Predict the future. I was more than intrigued. I was aghast, in awe, shocked that I didn't know this, had never been told this, nor taught this. I almost felt cheated!

So then of course more questions come to mind. I was totally intrigued, the most important question then finally presented itself in my life, did that mean God was real after all????? Just the idea seemed absurd, to say out loud " God is real " would make me laugh. It was against everything I had ever believed, against everything I ever thought was true, my whole world was turned upside down.

For weeks I thought about it, and turned the idea over and over in my head. Slowly letting the concept of God being real set in, it brought a huge smile to my face, I was endlessly amazed. I was very glad I had always been wrong. I'd always felt there was something I was missing that there was more to life. I just didn't realise the truth had been right there all along, that I was just too ignorant to realise it. I watched more documentaries. I was still a long way away from going to church, and religion seemed a horrible idea. But more and more my belief grew, my belief in God.

A couple of months passed then the most amazing thing happened something, I was not prepared for or even knew that could happen. I heard the voice of God, giving me the answer I so desperately needed, why I was so sick.

I was sitting there on my couch, and glanced at the packet of antidepressant I so diligently took daily, placed on the coffee table where they were kept so I didn't forget to take them. Alongside the packets of other pills, I took daily, prescribed by the doctors to keep me going.

The voice so clear in my head "That's what's making you sick".

Wait what, I was definitely confused, was that my own thought. It couldn't be, so clear, zero doubt, powerful, commanding, then the weight of those words sunk in, what they meant, the answer I so badly needed.

Get knotted I thought, as my emotions swirled and understanding took over. I'd been to sooooo many doctors and specialists over the years. NOT ONE had ever suggested that all the misery I was suffering, the gastritis, ulcers, nausea, overheating, dehydration and endless nightmares was SIDE EFFECTS from the antidepressants! I was horrified, a quick search on my phone showed 100% that that was exactly my problem, with the overheating and dehydration only more recently being published as side effects, with the gastrointestinal problems being the number one side effect! Actual words and explanations of what had been happening to me. I was aghast not one doctor had ever made this connection. I HAD BEEN POISONING MYSELF!

All the people that thought I had a drug problem were right I did! A huugggeee problem, with the drugs my own doctor had prescribed me, I was furious and in total shock. What was supposed to have made my life better had completely wrecked it. I'd done this to myself, and it took the voice of God for me to realise.

They say cigarettes are the hardest drug to quit, after recently stopping smoking, I can 1000000% tell u they lie! Stopping antidepressants is a million times harder! Your brain has to totally recompute, it's just plain awful, torture even.

I knew I just couldn't stop taking them. SSRIs are dangerous to just stop taking cold turkey, funny that! Something that is supposed to help your mental health can actually destroy it. From November 2021 upon making this discovery, I slowly reduced the dosage, but wow I went totally crazy. My emotions were a roller-coaster, a horror house, swinging from extreme depression to the most horrible anxiety I had ever felt. I was a monster to live with, and if friends showed up at the house, I would ask them to leave. I didn't trust myself not to fly off the handle. My poor kids hid, avoided me. I was constantly saying sorry for flying off the handle, sorry for being so angry, that I wasn't angry at them, that I was angry at everything. I had a hair-trigger temper. I didn't know this person I had become, crazy angry one minute, crying crazy the next. I had to stop work training horses. I couldn't go near a horse; they especially were horrified at this new Nicole. My endless patience they had come to trust was now non-existent. I was an adult sized toddler. I was unpredictable, something I had never been before. It was the hardest thing I have ever been through, mental health wise, if the side effects hadn't been so life destroying, I would have 100% gone back on the antidepressants just to make it stop. To have my mind back, to have a minute of peace.

Did I try a different antidepressant in my desperation, yes fluoxetine is what they gave me, otherwise known as Prozac! How horrid that was, it was the opposite end of the extreme. I was a robot with no emotions, completely disassociated, sedated even, tripping over my own feet, stuff that! I stopped them after a week. I've since come to be aware how often this drug is prescribed to people, especially to teenagers, it's truly horrifying how it can potentially affect you.

Physically I'd spent years making an income from my body training the horses. I was self-aware and coordinated, all that went out the window on Prozac. It just wasn't worth the break from the crazy roller coaster of emotion I was on, so I battled on. I cared for horses living here, but still wasn't ready to resume actually training them. I needed me back first.

By February I was medication free, but the mental side was worse than ever, the evil voice was whispering suicide, climb on the roof it said, jump it said. It felt like that would have been much easier at the time. But by nature, I'm very stubborn, so there was no way I was going to listen to that voice, which was nothing like God. It was a nasty bully voice in my head. I blocked her out the best I could, and refused to listen. I was strong enough to know that suicide was never going to happen. I just knew I needed to shut her up, evict her!

For someone that's never experienced depression or anxiety, the best way to explain it is there is a voice in your head that's really nasty, they know all your weaknesses, all your faults. Every wrong thing you have ever done, every mistake, every humiliation, and it taunts you, it's a nasty bully that goes on and on and on, day and night. It's just plain torture, people commit suicide to escape it, which can be understandable at times. I was getting desperate to shut her up as well.

Then there's the other side of Depression the weight, like a heavy blanket that you are carrying around suffocating you, like a heavy rock that is sitting on your head, the horrible oppressive feeling, the exhaustion, the wanting to hide in sleep so you don't have to feel or to listen to that voice anymore to carry that weight.

Anxiety is depression's evil best mate, you so badly want to do something, even something simple like go buy bread, but then you pick it apart, break it down into 1000 steps, so even the simplest tasks become a huge mountain that feels impossible to climb. Giving up and retreating feels like the only option, then someone tries to help, by pushing or encouraging you, wanting to help, and self-preservation comes out. The feeling you need to defend yourself, the feeling they are attacking you, making you feel even more worthless, that you can't even get the smallest task achieved, the feeling of being judged and misunderstood. To stop the feeling overwhelms you. You need it to stop, you want them to back away to leave you alone, so you get angry and lash out, but then the guilt and shame kicks in. It is a horrible cycle, and it's just as terrible for those around you, those that care, as it is for you, but you don't realise this at the time, often just wanting to be left alone, to retreat into yourself.

Round and round you go, literally beating yourself to a pulp in your own mind, desperate to escape, managing your whole life so as to try to avoid those feelings and thoughts, the bottomless pit.

But this time was different, this time I had the realization that God was real. I finally had someone to ask for help, and ask for help I did, actually beg is probably closer to the truth. I begged God for help from the endless misery that is depression and anxiety, but my understanding, wisdom and faith weren't quite there yet. First the flood would come, then the miracle would happen.

Lessons Learnt...

God used horses to teach me many lessons, these would help my journey building a relationship with Him, before I knew Him.

My journey with God feels like it has come out of no-where, and moved very fast, but looking back, it has always felt like there has been a guiding hand on my life, especially when you take into account all the supernatural things that have happened. I give full credit to God now I understand, and have wisdom of the truth.

My horse journey always felt like it happened by accident, but it wasn't an accident at all, it was God preparing me for when I finally believed to be able to get to know Him, to hear Him and to follow the narrow path with the wisdom already gained over so many years working with horses.

So many lessons of life, God used horses to teach me first, lessons learnt the hard way, wisdom gained that now has a new perspective, and I can carry through into the future.

Praise God, thank you for bringing me to you, now I finally understand, please continue to show me the way. Here are those lessons:

LESSON A

Communication with observation

> "Whatever I command You, be careful to observe it; you shall not add to it nor take away from it." Deuteronomy 12:32 NKJ

Hearing from God usually does not involve words, there may be a thought placed in your mind, or an image, but often it is through His word and the world around us that God communicates. We must be very observant, we must pay attention to what is going on around us, we must look for the signs and symbols that God shows us as answers to our questions. We must then use our own discernment to understand if this is from God, or a trick of evil to divert us of God's path.

Horses are not an animal that uses sound as a tool of communication very often, they very much use body language, this requires a great deal of observation. We must be constantly paying attention, the flick of an ear in a different direction, the wrinkles around the eyes, or the flair of the nostrils are all ways in which the horse is communicating with us. It is very important to listen, look and feel the horse's communication in order to help them overcome their worries and keep ourselves safe. Missing a small signal from a horse can lead to a horse needing to communicate in a much larger more dangerous way, like learning to listen to the Lord, it keeps us safe and on the right path.

LESSON B

Focus on the good not the bad

> "Finally, brothers, whatever is true, whatever is noble, whatever is right, whatever is pure, whatever is lovely, whatever is admirable- if anything is excellent or praiseworthy- think about such things. Whatever you have learned or received or heard from me seen in me – put into practice." Philippians 4: 4-9 NIV

There will be many hurdles both in our God journey and our horse one, it is so easy to get caught up where we are at present, especially when things are hard and going wrong. We may not be sleeping due to nightly spiritual attacks, or maybe every electronic device you own is malfunctioning at the same time. We start to feel negative, slip into the why me, have depression start to take over, feel like the weight of the world is suddenly on our shoulders, but it's at these times its important to focus on the good not the bad.

We must bring our minds into giving thanks for the things we do have, to remember how far we have come already. As we progress to learning more about God, Jesus and the Holy Spirit, to becoming more like Jesus, as the spiritual attacks get worse, we must remember how far we have already come, how much we have changed for the good, not let this bump in the road, a Satan trick, make us forget how far we have progressed along the narrow path, how much God has already blessed us, how much victory against evil we have already had.

The horse journey also has many bumps, a horse which has been progressing may all of a sudden decide he's having a bad day, and not want to be caught, or do something he has never done before. But horses taught me we must always stay positive, we must not forget how many bumps we have already navigated, how much the horse has already learnt and improved. The further along the journey the easier it is to see, but in those moments it's easy to lose hope, to focus on what's going wrong, but this gets us nowhere and only brings us down, which is never helpful. We must focus on the good, take a step back if we need to, have a rest and remember we are blessed, and there's always tomorrow.

Chapter 4

FLOOD VISIONS. PROOF OF GOD

It was now March 2022, I was really struggling mentally, I didn't feel like myself at all, my anxiety was easily triggered, and my temper was short. When it comes to working with horses, you need to be calm with endless patience. I didn't know myself anymore and had stopped taking client horses, only helping a few friends and working with my own. Sadly, needing to sell most just to stay afloat financially over the coming year.

But I had heard God's voice, and had a growing faith which gave me hope, something to hold onto. At least I finally had an answer to my physical health issues after so long.

The year before, March 2021 we had experienced a flood for the first time in the 14years of living here. My horse training business had then been in full swing then, even though my own health was shocking, with ulcers, gastritis and what I now know was permanent dehydration and overheating multiple times a day. I had soldiered on. I hadn't realised yet the antidepressants were the cause for me being physically exhausted and a total mess health wise. I just kept working and doing my best, I didn't know what else to do.

When the first flood arrived in 2021, I was very blessed when a close neighbour 2 doors up the hill, offered to take the horses. There were 10 here at the time, both my own and agistment horses. This was a relatively simple move, 200m up the street to higher ground and to safety, which we could do on foot, leading the horses. She was also great helping to feed them as well, especially when water rose higher, and we were doing what we could at the house to move our belongings.

But this flood in March 2022, was to be very different. The 10 horses evacuated to the neighbours property the year before, was a lot, and with all of the rain they had damaged her paddocks, so when it looked like we were going to flood again, and needed to evacuate she said no to helping. Which meant I needed to move the now 6 horses somewhere else. Not such a simple exercise, with a couple of horses that needed to be walked out, due to fear of horse floating, and the constant rain hammering down. I'm also nervous and not very experienced at towing a horse float, and my float being small meant that only one horse at a time could be moved, and to where I still did not know.

With me already struggling both mentally and physically, this turn of events was something that almost broke me. My anxiety exploded, mentally I was almost paralysed, not knowing what to do or whom to ask for help, nor where to put the horses. I felt very alone with others relying on me. Yet I could barely string a sentence together. I felt like the 10years of antidepressants had scrambled my brain now I had stopped taking them. I didn't feel like myself, and making any sort of decision was a nightmare. Hopelessness overcame me many times. Dark waves which felt like drowning, and my physical health was still far from good. My body still broken.

The thing with flood warnings is they are just that, warnings, there is no guarantee a flood will actually arrive, so I could be stressing for nothing. Which honestly makes things worse, your brain goes around and around, like an out-of-control merry-go-round, actually more like a blender!

Do I move the horses or not? Do we start the massive job of moving everything in the shed to higher ground? I felt sick in body and mind, totally overwhelmed in bed crying and exhausted, not able to make any decision at all, doubt hammering me at every attempt to decide.

I now understand why in the moments we are the most exhausted, in our greatest desperation and turmoil, are the moments people turn to God. God had shown up in my desperation to understand what had been making me so physically ill, then why not when I again was desperate for an answer, when I was at rock bottom, broken.

So plead with God I did. "God what do I do?" In a crying crazy mess type ask, not a quiet moment type ask. Basically, one huge HELP! On my knees begging type ask.

This time it wasn't a voice that said, "that's what is making you sick." This time it was an image that came into my head, and is still burned on my brain today. An image that was a bit strange, so as to make an impression and catch my attention, enough to know that it was not of me. Not something I imagined myself.

The way my house is laid out, my bedroom is on the 3rd story; the whole house is actually on piers 3m off the ground. It was quite common for me to keep the horses around the house, in the yard, to eat the grass. It is also the highest place on the property. In the year previously, this area had remained high enough so that the flood waters did not reach it, while all the paddocks had flooded. It was somewhere the horses would be safe, and wouldn't need to be evacuated, if only the water didn't come higher than the year before. But with floods you just don't know, they are very different from a fire, they creep up slowly, a huge massive unstoppable power that you cannot fight. You have no idea when they will stop rising and slowly retreat back the way they came, leaving everything a wet muddy stinky mess, reminding you of their visit. While at the same time there is a scary beauty to the immense volume of water, as it arrives and then the rain stops. Huge trees engulfed, the power of God very much on display.

I was sitting on my bed at the time God sent me my answer. The image that came into my mind was as if the house was invisible all of a sudden, as if I could see through the walls and floor, to places I couldn't see in real life sitting on my bed. I was looking down at the horses grazing from above. It took me a minute to understand the perspective, understand what I was seeing. Longer to understand what this image meant, that this was a gift from God, a vision of the future. That I was being shown that it would be fine to not evacuate the horses, that the water wouldn't rise higher than last flood, that I could breathe for a moment. That everything would be alright.

I grabbed this image with all my might, all my hope as truth. Truth from God. It definitely took all my growing faith, but against human advice I chose to keep the horses here, to stop my own panic, to trust the vision. As the rain continued to fall and the water rose, I prayed that it would be ok. I held onto my faith in God with all that I had.

The vision was of course 100% correct. The rain stopped, the waters rose and rose, but the area I saw horses in the vision standing, remained untouched as the flood peaked, and 48hrs later the water started to recede. I felt a huge sense of relief, as if I had been given a huge blessing. I collapsed at the feet of God saying Thank you, Thank you, Thank you Lord.

But then a week later the worst happened, and rain started again, the weather report said much more rain was predicted. Again, the water started to rise. My heart clenched, my anxiety shot up, the panic set in. Again, I begged for God's help, to tell me what to do, did I need to evacuate, what should I do? help me, Lord.

Again, God heard my pleas, another vision came, but this time the image I got wasn't what I wanted to see, this time I saw four white horses, tied to the fence up the road on much higher ground.

Panic set in. I needed to move 6 horses and so much stuff that was stored under the house and in the shed. The rain poured down, I had nowhere to take the horses yet.

But God made sure I heard, and knew to act, and not wait, not second guess the vision. The following morning my son came to me, said he had a dream that the water would rise much higher than it had done before, and the areas that had been dry would now be under over a metre of water.

This is exactly what came to pass. The four horses I had seen in my vision ended up being 4 white cars, parked on higher ground up the street. God knew I would know exactly what those 4 white horses up the hill would mean, just like he knew I would understand what seeing the horses still at the house meant we were safe. He then sent my son the dream, to make sure I would have no doubt, as confirmation that I had the answer to my question, to my prayers, while there was still the time. I needed to act fast, as it would only be 72 hrs before the water would win, and act I did, getting horses moved just in time to be safe.

Among all the stress and all the chaos, something in me now knew that it wasn't for nothing. In all this chaos, my world had changed forever, my faith and my belief in God had started to grow exponentially. God had given me further proof he was real. Tangible confirmation, proof the world wasn't just what we see, smell, hear and touch. An understanding that there actually was something more, something supernatural, something greater than us. Now I knew exactly what that was, God. The tiny mustard seed had started to sprout and take root, little did I know how big that tree would grow.

Lessons Learnt...

LESSON C

To not get offended.

> "Good sense makes one slow to anger, and it is His glory to overlook an offense." Proverbs 19:11 ESV

This is an important lesson the Bible wants us to learn, we are not supposed to take offense. Offence torments us, makes us angry, which opens doors for oppression, we get bitter and take our eyes off God, losing our peace and joy. Not a good place to be.

When working with horse's things go wrong. It is never a straight line; you must never become offended if a horse freaks out and reacts to protect itself from fear or pain. Though sadly this is often seen, a horse bucks someone off, and the human gets offended and punishes the horses. Hits the horse, blames the horses, they are quick to anger. Horses are just not wired this way; we must learn to never be offended. I'm glad to say this was never my way, not being offended by humans is a much harder lesson to learn, but like everything from God, brings peace of mind.

LESSON D

Obey

> "As obedient children, do not be conformed to the passions of your former ignorance." 1 Peter 1:14 ESV

This is less a horse lesson more a God lesson. God asks so little from us, but when he sends us a message, he wants us to obey. Society these days wants us to feel we should do whatever we want, whatever makes us feel happy or good, to think we should never obey. But it is so misunderstood, it's for our own good, but it brings us immense blessings, immense joy, the fear of God is wanting to obey out of love.

Being mentored in my horse journey, I was given advice to follow. I was never expected to obey, but this advice was best followed, for my own good, given with good intent, to keep me safe, to help the horse. Advice given from experience as wisdom, the same intent God has, our Father who wants nothing but the best for us. We should obey, even when we don't understand why, the why is revealed in hindsight, and is always for ours or the horse's best.

Chapter 5

DELIVERED FROM DEPRESSION, THE BEGINNING OF WISDOM

The floods came and went, I was still in shock and awe about the visions God had given me. The fact that my prayers had been answered. I had moved the horses just in time, even leading 2 through thigh high flood water at one stage. But everyone was safe, although we had again lost thousands of dollars' worth of possessions and were left with a huge stinky muddy mess. It's heartbreaking and cleaning up takes weeks, everything gets put on hold as you are trying to get back to normal. It would only be 3 months before another even bigger flood would come rolling in, but ignorance is bliss as we cleaned up.

For me there was now no going back, everything was different, normal would never be the same again. God was real and there was zero questioning that now, zero doubt, my faith was as solid as a rock and could not be shifted. I now knew where to find the truth after all these years of wondering. I could now grasp it. I had somewhere to look for answers. Not just questions, questions and more questions and wondering where the truth was. Now I knew the truth and my learning adventure could begin, the beginning of wisdom

Of course the Bible is the obvious place to start but I didn't even own a Bible! In these situations, the internet is a huge blessing. To start I found cartoon versions of all the Bible stories, the Bible project, and spent hours listening to the stories in each book. Wondering how I never knew so many of these in the first place, especially after 13 years of catholic schooling.

Learning about God is endless. People spend their whole lives studying. I discovered questions I never knew I had, the Bible is no normal book, so many layers of learning. The way the answers to one section is found in another, in books written by people that lived hundreds of years apart, who never met. Stories of giants of the past, mighty men. I was shocked at the violence, the evil, how whole populations would be wiped out. How everyone made mistakes, there was so much I didn't understand.

One discovery that I made early on that was life changing was that of the 3 voices in our head:

> Our own
> Gods
> And Satan

This explained a lot of what had been going on in my own head, that nasty bully voice that I always felt disconnected from was never in fact my own. The mean bitchy voice that knew all my weaknesses and secrets, was in fact trying to bring me down. It wanted me scared, depressed, anxious, guilty, shamed, angry, jealous. All the worst emotions that exist, the feelings I had been trying to run from, that tormented me. It wanted me out destroying myself with sin.

I learnt that the Bible said to edit our thoughts, but that is easier said than done. That voice in my head, the nasty cruel one seemed to be getting louder and louder, especially now I wasn't taking the antidepressants, which did seem to keep it at bay. Now that I believed God was real, I'd really aggravated the evil voice, it knew what I didn't know, and was taking full advantage. I'd walked straight into the middle of a war I hadn't even known existed and I was getting my butt kicked, a full-blown spiritual attack.

They say Satan's greatest trick is making people believe he is not real; they are not wrong. He's cunning, devious, genius smart and hates us more than we can ever imagine. He will use every trick in the book to keep us away from God, to keep us distracted, to busy and tied up in human affairs, to realise there is a bigger picture. He wants us to think we are in control, that there is nothing outside us influencing us. He wants us to think all the thoughts in our head are our own, that we are bad people thinking bad thoughts. That the choices we make and the sins we commit don't matter. That we are just flesh, evolved from monkeys over millions of years, an accident of nature that grew a brain. That our own pleasure and being happy is what we should be concerned about, is the most important goal to reach.

Satan wants us to think that we are not accountable to God. That there is no heaven or hell, he wants us to think we need to be rich and successful. He wants us to strive for beauty, to be skinny and fit, to have others want to be like us. He wants us to think we need to be winners. He wants us to give our bodies away, to be sexual beings, sleeping with whomever we choose, because it makes us feel good in the moment. He wants us to be wanted. He wants us to not worry about the cost, he wants us to think there is no cost. He wants us to think we have no soul.

When we do start to realise there is more. He wants us to go down the new age track, crystals, astrology, star signs, star children, tarot cards, energy healing, witch craft, voodoo, magic, reiki, and much more. The list is long, something for everyone, or if we take up one of the religions, he wants us to find one that idolises a deity or human like Hinduism, Buddhism, Islam, Scientology anything but Jesus.

Satan wants us to idolise a job or another human, a pop star or a movie star. He has tricked us into having idols and worship through entertainment. He wants us to curse ourselves, with music and words, and speak blasphemy as part of our everyday language, without realising what we speak. He wants us drinking, taking drugs that alter our minds to make us feel better, to think that is the answer to finally finding peace and joy. He wants us to think we are sick, not tricked. But most of all he wants us to be sinners and never ever give our lives to Jesus and be saved. As the Bible says the path is narrow, he wants us not to walk that way. He wants us on an endless search for peace and joy, to be always going the wrong way, away from God.

I was beyond miserable, tormented was an understatement. I'd never felt so low. I didn't understand why. I was always on the verge of tears or an angry outburst. I felt like I was being eaten alive by evil. I didn't know how to escape, if the antidepressants hadn't had such huge physical side effects, I would have gladly taken them again, just to get a break to make this torment stop, to shut up my mind, that evil voice.

There's an easy way out the voice would tell me, climb on the roof and jump, terrible advice! Though I can understand why people listen, me, I'm stubborn, not so easily convinced, perhaps not brave enough either. Suicide was just never an option, and I was starting to understand that was a one-way ticket to hell, another trick. When people say they are struggling with their demons, they don't know how right they are.

I was spending too much time in bed. I didn't want to see anyone. I isolated myself. I cried and I cried. I couldn't see an end in sight, everything felt hopeless, but as I continued to learn about God and the devil. I grew in wisdom.

I held onto the hope of what God represented with every fibre of my being. The learning path in itself felt like God guiding me, guiding what I was viewing on the internet, what the endless scroll showed me. More and more pieces of the puzzle started to fall into place, when I didn't even know what a was looking for. I was still a new born baby in terms of what I knew, in Christianity, but keep learning, I did, searching desperately for answers, for wisdom, for freedom from my mind.

I was slowly understanding how God talks to us, trying to discern the voices in my head, war war war, seemed to be a constant word I would get. I just needed to learn how to fight, but what were my weapons? I really didn't understand, but God has a plan and His timing always works out in ways our human brains can never comprehend.

I would ask and people would tell me "Oh God already won the war" but that didn't make sense, when I felt like I was in the middle of a huge battle. I wasn't going to back down, turn away from God, but I sure was taking a lot of hits, how could I protect myself?

I knew the Word, the Bible, was a weapon, our sword, but I didn't really understand how the Word was a weapon, how the armour of God worked. I still didn't own a Bible. I didn't know how to pray. worship music seemed very strange. The idea of going to church, I was still extremely resistant too. I had a long way to go.

But I had made the biggest leap of my life, I believed, I was willing to give my life to God, to surrender. But Satan knew this and would try his hardest to stop me, push me off the path, to make me use my free will to turn and run from God.

I was still so very tormented, I would have done anything for the torment in my head to stop, to have that horrible weight lifted off me. God had heard me when I begged for help with the floods, maybe if I begged enough God could make this voice in my head shut up. Help me win my own part in the war.

Then amongst all this learning, God finally figured I had enough understanding and growing wisdom, that I'd proved I had enough faith, that I was on the right path, and I was guided to videos about Deliverance.

I don't remember the video I watched. I was watching so many different things at that time, and was obsessed with Bible prophecy. My mind constantly absorbed in how everything was coming together, the realisation we were in end times, the meaning of rapture, and what that could mean for the world and myself, my family and friends.

Deliverance was a big part of Jesus ministry, the new covenant, the video of deliverance taught me the idea that you could evict evil spirts from your mind and body. How the word was a weapon, that these demons were that weight I was carrying around, that I was sure I could feel resting on the top on my head, that heavy blanket I had talked about for years that I was carrying around. That voice in my head, my tormentors, the nasty mean bullies in my mind. Jesus gifted us the power to get rid of all of them, to be free.

God blessed me mightily that night, gave me great wisdom, a key, two words were all it took. ELOHIEM, OUT! I said them out loud and just like that God delivered me from depression and anxiety. I felt something leave. I didn't quite understand what had happened at first. It would never be that simple again, but God has power to do anything, anytime, anyhow, and he answered my endless begging for help. He handed me a weapon he knew I would pick up and learn how to use. Like learning to train horses I would learn until I understood and could wield the weapon. Till I had the wisdom, till I could use it myself, go after the enemy, while giving Him all the glory. God knows our heart; I had proved worthy.

To my astonishment, over the following days it sank in more and more, the realisation it was gone, the depression and anxiety had lifted. I had been delivered, that nasty mean bully voice which had been with me for as long as I could remember, that I was told was part of me, a medical condition that ran in my family, a chemical imbalance was gone, evicted, just like that, the silence it left was quite amazing. I would pause hold my breath waiting for it to kick in again, nope, wow wow wow yay go God! Praise Jesus thank you thank you thank you.

It still shocks me the depression and anxiety are gone, not to say the voice of evil is gone completely. I'm still flesh, the down feeling the doubts and worries and sadness of being human kick back in. That's why the Bible says edit your every thought, that demon that horrid spirit of depression and anxiety, that weight which took over my mind was gone, that weight I carried for years, was evicted. I was free! Hallelujah.

I was off and running then, empowered by God. I wanted to understand the how, what, why is deliverance. What exactly had happened, where could I learn more, where could I get more. I finally had a weapon, a feeling I could fight back, it was uplifting, freeing, a huge blessing.

Over the coming weeks it really sank in for the first time, and I really felt it, the most important thing, the most significant thing I would ever learn, the greatest realisation of life:

JESUS LOVES ME.

JESUS died on the cross so I could be free of the evils of oppression. He loves me so much that he died for me, more love than I could comprehend, hooray! PRAISE JESUS. I could literally feel it. I danced around the happiest I've ever felt, a taste of the peace and joy only God can bring.

Did that high last forever, no not like the initial high, that hug from God, the Holy Spirit. Satan has more war tactics than me! But I'd felt what

I now knew to be the goal, the narrow path, the feeling of the love of Jesus, and that was where I knew I wanted to be.

Some of my biggest revelations would come over the following weeks and months, they were numerous, and life changing:

- Realising you could feel the Holy Spirit, that feeling when all your hair stands on end, learning how he was my best friend, how much he wanted to help.
- Understanding of how the devil worked, that evil voice inside my head, a feeling that could bring me down. How his power over me came from a legal system I needed to learn, and how sin gave legal rights to torment me, even sin from past generations.
- The power of the words we speak over ourselves and others, we must be so cautious, or we leave an open door for demons.
- All the different types of evil spirits that could attack me, depression being just one of many.
- That God loves to use a broken person, the Bible is full of God using broken people, of their lives being turned around.
- That humans are not just good or bad. we are being influenced spiritually by a much larger force, a world of dark powers.
- That the main goal of life is a relationship with God, making God proud of me mattered above everything, it was the greatest purpose.
- The Bible is the manual for life, I just needed to learn how it put all this knowledge to good use, gain the wisdom to understand it.
- Hearing God, and having God show me the way, was everything.

Most importantly:

- That Jesus loved me, despite my mistakes and past. I was forgiven, a new creation.

There was still so much more to learn. Prayer still felt awkward and unnatural. I said the 'Our Father' which I remember from school over and over. I spoke to God all day long, every time I stumbled and sinned even just swearing, I repented. I said thankyou many times every day. My relationship with God slowly grew.

Learning about deliverance, I first came across one of the grand fathers of modern deliverance. Derek prince. I watched videos and took notes, understanding that the spiritual world was a court of law.

I also learnt Satan had legal rights to torment us whenever we sinned. We are all sinners, only Jesus was perfect.

The ways in which Satan would torment us occurred in 3 ways, different demons and spirits for different sins:

1. Oppression demons: these demons are voices in our heads, they tell us lies, give us doubts, confuse us, depress us and give us anxiety, they send mind arrows into our souls to bring us down, torment us.
2. Attachment demons: these demons trigger us to anger, rage, annoyance, lies, violence, hate, all the things we don't like about ourselves.
3. Possession demons: these are less seen and come when we give our lives to Satan through rituals, Satanism, occult, witchcraft, blood, when we make a conscious choice to take up idols.

Even with knowledge of all of these demons Satan sends to destroy us, to torment us, to make us miserable, it is easy to underestimate how much Satan hates us, his dripping clawing hate, he wants us to join him in hell, he thrives on our misery.

All this learning was shocking but also enlightening in my growing wisdom. The world I lived in, why things were the way they were, started to make a lot more sense. A tactic of war is to know thy enemy and I was definitely learning just that. I learnt that Jesus' death on the cross meant the final round of the war was won. That He would return to collect His warriors, His bride, to inflict the final blow. But surviving the battle that raged around me before his return was what I needed to do. I read resist the devil and he would flee. But how?

The more I learned, the more I discovered about the enemy. How although he didn't know the future, he was watching, he had spies, monitoring spirits. How he waited and used our weaknesses against us, even in sleep we were not safe, he could not read our minds, but he heard our words and would use them against us where ever possible.

He could also appear in the physical world, and those ghosts I had seen so many years before hand, were more than likely demons, sent to scare me when I was already terrified. Fear being a favourite trick of evil, the opening of a door, a legal right.

It made me wonder about "the knowing" had God been trying to warn me, send me a clue about the trouble ahead. If Satan didn't know the future it had to be God, was he allowing me to see into the spiritual world, see things occur in the spiritual world before they occurred in the physical. A prophetic warning? a lesson I would come to learn later when the dreams started.

But for now, all my attention was on deliverance. I wrote out what I thought was the basic formula, and all the Bible verses to accompany it. I was still yet to own a Bible, but it wouldn't be long. A friend whose mother had passed recently, was clearing out some belongings, she came across a Bible and gifted to me, my first Bible since high school. God is good all the time, all the time God is good.

The basic formula for deliverance, I had learnt, and by this stage I'd been researching for months, trying to get my head around it, and understand my own authority, how it all worked, if God would allow me to do it again:

Dear Lord.

1. Praise God.

    Give gratitude and thanks for life, love, family, friends, nature, peace, safety, the list is endless follow your heart.
2. Confess.

    Repent and renounce your sins, anger, hate, greed, lies, vanity, gluttony, self-destruction, curses, soul ties, witchcraft, again the list is long. Satan will use any sin to send demons for us to make life harder, more miserable, more fearful, anything negative is not from God.
3. Deliver.

    With the authority of the power and the blood of Jesus, the name of Jesus, command the demons, by name if needed, to go to Jesus. To get out, to leave, to go to the abyss never to return. As it is finished, in the name of Jesus.

You must do this with the Holy Spirit by your side, understanding your own authority, and rights in the name of Jesus, without backing down. I was still a baby Christian, but knew I was on the right path, the narrow path, where God wanted me to be.

But I was still quite unsure, not knowing if I could just go ahead and start trying to evict more demons from myself. I kept researching and finding more and more videos. With my interest the things of my old life, such as watching TV and movies, slowly wanning. I was instead watching hours of vids about deliverance, Bible prophecy and understanding the

Bible. I was shocked at the change in myself. I was truly reborn, and would continue to be.

Over the next six months, I also started to throw things out from my life before Jesus, things I had collected over the years, from my travels overseas, things I had thought were harmless, such as an abstract painting of the karma sutra, done on silk, and a small mirror covered elephant purchased in India, anything that might give Satan a foothold in my life, a legal right, out they went, renounced and thrown in the trash. Did I miss things? Yes! But it wasn't til later, that things, less obvious such as a Stephen king book I'd missed collecting dust in a draw would really come back to bite me, there were so many traps.

It was now maybe 7 or 8 months since God had miraculously delivered me from depression and anxiety, life had been a roller-coaster, but my mind had improved so much after 10 years of antidepressant poison, I was growing to love God more and more every day.

But my physical health wasn't good, but the side effects from the antidepressants such as ulcers and gastritis had improved. I wasn't overheating, but my weight was dropping, my body hurt, my joints ached and the psoriasis on my skin was again covering most of my body. I was so very tired all the time. I was really struggling to get through life. I had still not returned to training client horses, and the progressive sale of my own horses was the only thing keeping us going financially. I had one more horse to sell, once those funds ran out, I would be in trouble.

Being a parent can come with a lot of guilt, my twins were now 15. and I felt like a failure as a parent. After years of not wanting to leave the house due to being sick, then going crazy coming off the antidepressants, now there was a new thing, me being exhausted mentally and physically. I felt like I was never doing enough as a mother, that I wasn't there for them as a mother. After my own disconnected childhood, I didn't want that for my own children, my own mother had spoken guilt over me as a sick child, adding to that weight. The shame and guilt of being an inconvenience to others, shame and guilt eats away at you, and Satan is happy to throw a party and encourage these things. I needed to get free.

Finally, I decided to try using all my new wisdom, and do deliverance on myself. Because God would never make me feel like this, so it must be a tactic of the enemy! Time to evict those demons and trust in God that things would get better, that he would show me the way forward.

In saying that the Bible isn't a Disney story, the most blessed people in the Bible like David or Job go through the greatest trials, the hardest times, but never ever do they turn away or lose trust in God. I now knew this, and understood I just had to keep going, give it all to God! Breakthrough would come eventually.

I don't remember the exact date, it was mid-morning, the TV was blaring in the back ground so nobody else could hear me. I felt a bit embarrassed as I really was jumping in with 2 feet, hoping this was Gods path, not wanting to be interrupted.

I started with shame. I thanked the Lord for as much as I could think of, His mercy and grace, my friends, family, horses, home life.

Then I called out the demon of shame, repenting for my shame, renouncing shame, binding shame, casting shame out to the pit in the name and the blood of Jesus. Over and over, I said this calling on my authority, commanding it, knowing that Jesus' death gave me this authority.

And then it started to happen, my stomach started to turn. I started to cough; my mouth watered so bad I need to spit it out. I burped a lot! I coughed a lot more, over and over I kept saying out, I kept evicting the demon of shame out, casting it out to the pit, in the name and blood of Jesus out!

My logical brain doubted what was happening, but my spirit was stronger. Over and over, 10 min then 20, then 30 mins passed. I wasn't sure if it was gone. I renounced again and this time nothing, then I felt it. The Holy Spirit filling my body with the amazing peace and joy that can only come from God. Whoop whoop I danced around the lounge, celebrating the great love of Jesus. A great blessing from God.

Then off I went again evicting guilt this time, over and over I repeated the words, stepped into my authority. Once more did the coughing and gagging start, then out it went, sent to the abyss, the pit, in Jesus' name. Such a relief another weight lifted. Those 2 tormentors' shame and guilt are a nasty pair, I was very glad to be rid of after a lifetime of their oppression, and now I just had to keep editing my thoughts. If they tried to creep back in, I had to block and ignore and repent. They were not welcome; the door was closed. I wanted to do better, be better, have a better future not to live in the past. I had to believe I was forgiven. I was reborn in God, a new creation.

I think one of the hardest things about getting delivered, is admitting what you need freedom from, to yourself. A lot of people would be quick to deny they feel shame, or perhaps the way they have treated others even in a moment of anger, or the way they had shame spoken over them, or the guilt they feel about a choice they made. Even when things were out of their control, or they felt they were doing the right thing at the time, they get defensive self-righteous, pride kicks in, and they lose their chance at freedom. But only Jesus was perfect, we all have something, some demon inside us.

I was amazed, the exhaustion of shame and guilt had lifted. I could stop beating myself about things from the past. I had so much gratitude to be given this gift again, this key, the power to throw off these sins to cast out these demons, to tread on snakes and scorpions, to walk in the power that

Jesus gifted to the saved when he gave himself as living sacrifice, defeating evil, tricking Satan himself. I was again blessed with a battle I had won, praise Jesus! Praise Jesus! The excitement bubbled up in me, my weapon of war had been wielded. God was guiding me, blessing me. I had no idea what the future held, but God was in control. "Show me the way God" became my mantra. I give my life to you Lord, I surrender.

Lessons Learnt...

LESSON E

Capture every thought.

> "We take captive every thought to make it obedient to Christ." 2 Corinthians 10:5 NIV

I used to call this cancel delete, working with unpredictable horses, with a past of being dangerous, can be hard on the mind. It is easy to let your brain run away from you, to start thinking of all the scenarios where something can go wrong, how you will get hurt.

The way I learnt to overcome this, was to recognise my own thoughts as soon as my mind tried to think down that road. I would capture the thought and then "cancel delete" that thought. This takes some practice, but over the years was something that was much more automatic, well-practiced.

This has had a huge benefit now I understand my own mind better, now I understand the whispers of evil. I apply this lesson to Satan's words, any thoughts that are not from God. Such as worry or annoyance or frustration, anything not from God. I recognise it and "cancel delete". I stop myself from thinking those thoughts as best I can, this is much harder than it was with the horse thoughts. But because I am well practiced, I try to apply it constantly. As the Bible says, every thought must be tested, it very much helps to keep the peace and joy of my mind. There are days when I fail, but that's when I repent, renounce, apologise to God, get my mind back on track, obedient to Christ, where true happiness lives.

LESSON F

Self-awareness and being accountable

> "Examine yourselves, to see whether you are in the faith. Test yourselves. Or do you not realize this about yourselves that Jesus Christ is in you? – unless indeed you fail to meet the test!" Corinthians 13:5 ESV

Self-awareness and accountability on the God journey is something that develops along the way. You so much want to please God; this means you become much stricter with yourself. You do not want to make a decision or act in any way that would lead to sin, nor disappoint God. Even watching horror movies becomes something to be avoided, as it allows Satan to come in and plant a seed in our minds that can grow and torment us. Which as we become more self-aware, we notice more and more, we want to maintain our peace and joy, which requires us to be accountable to our actions and thoughts, to test who we are, this is the path of wisdom that God provides if we ask and pray for it.

When we do make a wrong decision or action, we must be accountable, this can bring some discomfort, we as humans often don't like to be wrong, nor admit we have made a mistake, but this is all a part of being humble, pleasing God. Admitting our own failings, most importantly never blaming God.

This lesson is very much needed when working with horses. We must always be accountable for our actions and decisions. We must never blame the horse when things don't go as we planned. We must be willing to admit if we have made a mistake, and go asking for help if we don't know how to resolve it. Many people are quick to blame others in the horse's past, never being accountable for the part they have played, this just blocks our learning journey, stops us gaining wisdom that would make our journey in the future easier. Horses have a knack of keeping us humble, as soon as we think we know a lot, a horse will come along and show us how little we know, and how much we still have to learn. Lessons worth learning if we are willing to be accountable.

The truth will set you free.

LESSON G

Feelings. Don't listen to them

> "A fool vents all his feelings, but a wise man holds them back." Proverbs 29:11 NKJ

Ultimately in our journey with God we must be careful about listening to our feelings, especially feelings that are not of God.

Feelings get us in all sorts of trouble, frustration, anger, hate, jealousy, bitterness, lust, pride are only some examples that cause us to react in ways that are not beneficial to us, that take us away from God, from His promise of peace and joy. Most feelings are better ignored, as our growing self-awareness makes us more aware of our feelings, it gives us a greater chance to ignore them, not let Satan use them against us, to bring us trouble, cause us drama in our lives, and torment in our minds.

Feelings and acting on them, also do not help us in anyway with horses. It is best to shut them down, remain calm and consistent, this allows us to become predictable, and the horses then can trust us more and more. We won't have a sudden outburst of feelings that would make us unpredictable, dangerous, a thing to be wary of. This especially applies to horses that may have been abused by a person in the past who has lashed out, unable to control their own feelings. Taking out feelings on the horse that never had anything to do with the horse. If you want horses to trust you then you must be consistent in your own feelings, they do not count. A very worthwhile lesson to take from dealing with horses, to dealing with humans and life.

The Bible has the best advice, always!

Chapter 6

FELLOWSHIP BEGINS

Fellowship can be defined as:

> COMPANIONSHIP, COMPANY
> Looking for the fellowship of friendly people
> Community of interest, activity, feeling, or experience
> A company of equals or friends
> The quality or state of being comradely
> Meaningful communication for building
> trust and fellowship

I believe God points us in the direction of fellowship because it helps develop our relationship with Him, with Jesus and the Holy Spirit, it helps us understand we are not alone.

One of the highlights of working with horses has always been the amazing people I met along the way. Horses provide a common bond from which friendships are formed, and it was through horses that I met a couple of amazing women whom were walking their own God path. They both testified to me, but I was deaf to it at the time, though never forgot their stories, their testimony. They never bombarded me with preaching, just words of wisdom imparted here and there. It was many years before their words had an impact, but God placed them in my life no doubt so when I was finally ready to walk my own path, I would have someone to turn to, to tell, to say 'I found God' and have them be excited for me, to open the door for the next step, to allow God to bring me to Fellowship. Which would perhaps otherwise have taken much longer, as I had zero plans of ever going to church and did not understand the blessing of fellowship.

I had met Kris about 10 years beforehand when she bought a horse from me, we had kids the same age, both loved horses and she lived around the corner. Kris is an amazing woman, and has a huge group of friends, she would say it because she is a people pleaser, but I'd say it's because she's a good person who makes people feel comfortable, and is probably an evangelist at heart the way she draws people to where God needs them to be, so he can show up in their lives.

Amazingly enough she even convinced me to go to women's lunch group, Sisterhood, at her church many years ago. I went along purely out of curiosity. I was impressed by all the horse loving women and the food, less by any sort of Godly teaching, though I was fascinated by some of the testimonies given. No doubt planting a seed, it wasn't like any sort of church I'd known, but I only went a couple of times, at that stage in my life I was getting busier and busier with work and was becoming increasingly unwell.

Over the following years I ended up seeing less of Kris, she moved over the river and I basically stopped leaving the house. A trip 5 mins up the road became a stretch, anything further just didn't happen, and I got good at making excuses as to not offend people, rather than having to explain I was worried I would soil myself driving in the car so far. Even being at someone's house or out somewhere and needing to use the bathroom, then being gone for 30mins as you waited for cramps and cold sweat to pass, was something to be avoided at all costs. I've said previously I'm sure there was alot of people that thought I had some serious issues, whether it was mental health or drug related. I was a mess, I was drowning, and then I sank. Blessedly God then came charging in a on white horse and saved me, pulled me into the boat and strapped me in cause the biggest waves were still to come.

God has things planned way ahead of us, so off course the first person I told when I realised God was real in late 2021 was Kris!. She was one of the only Christians I knew; I've got no doubt she was probably as shocked as I was. I'd be the last person one would have put a bet on to find God. If God hadn't placed her in my life through horses all those years beforehand, I'm not sure who I would have told. I told my mother and she was pleased, relieved even, but she didn't have much knowledge to impart, and was definitely not a part of any church or fellowship, nor did she encourage me that that was what I needed. That the God path is not one that we should be walking alone, like she herself had been doing, which is a shame really, my mother missed out on so much by not having that community and learning, that guidance and understanding that needs to come from others, whom understand how to have a relationship with God. She lived in her own pit of depression, never finding freedom, the peace and joy of God.

I was just in the beginning of my journey of a relationship with God, and I certainly didn't understand fellowship til I found it, feeling I didn't need it. I was still close minded about needing others, stuck in the ideas of church, and the Bible I had grown up on. I certainly wouldn't have whole heartily given my life to God as I have done without more wisdom coming from others.

If God hadn't shown up when he did, then I really don't know where I would be now, and jumping of the roof may actually have started to seem like a good idea. Because if I thought things were bad with me before, when I was in the depths of illness then depression, then I was to learn just how bad they can get. But God was with me now, providing the hope I needed to survive and thrive in the darkest days, providing the people I needed at the time I needed them, putting me in the right place at the right time. with the right people.

God loves to use people in ways we don't even know are happening at the time. My telling Kris I had found God provided her with answers to questions I believe she had been asking. And that was upon deciding to leave her own church, to start a fellowship of women, outside the church, a group where women could share wisdom and provide the support and prayers so much needed in our lives today. To provide a safe non-judgemental space that women needed in our lives, as things get harder and trials come. Where people could crash and burn, and everyone else would pray and pick up the pieces. Where God could put them back together, stronger and more beautiful than they were before.

She very much achieved this, following Gods path no doubt with much success, as 4 women, close friends, strong Christian women came together and created Hope Hub. My initial inclination upon being invite was to run away, but I was so amused that they were having coffee in a bar that had previously been a church I went along, figuring it would do no harm, and that it was a much-needed path God was providing for me. This is where I was to learn that Gods path was never made to be walked alone, the power in multiples, of fellowship.

The initial meeting in late 2022 was myself and 5 others, all extremely lovely women, they didn't throw God in my face and were still trying to organise themselves about how they wanted everything to work. I myself was still a very very new baby Christian and clueless to how little I knew. But excited in what God was doing in my life. I remember bringing up learning about the power of singing the 'Our Father' prayer, and how God kept telling me "War, war, war". Worship you mean one of the ladies asked? That was what singing was ... worship! Huh? I didn't even know singing worship was a thing, or even understand worship at that stage. It seemed very foreign, the word worship conjured up the idea of idols and evil rather than God. I still wasn't comfortable with prayer, nor was I reading the Bible. The Bible felt overwhelming I didn't know where to even start, when I look how far I have come 12 months later, I'm quite shocked. God gave me the gift of learning, and learn I certainly have! The Bible is now my life manual.

God very much used the ladies to show me what I didn't know, that I needed fellowship, but it's only in hindsight do I understand this fully. I was just stumbling along learning as I went, never knowing what was to come next, or how significant these learnings would come to be later. The bigger picture the endless revelations that still come even today. God is good all the time. He has plans we know nothing about, he was leading me to church but I was clueless at the time, and would have stubbornly resisted if I did know!

Over time the group of women would grow significantly. God using these amazingly brave four women, who formed and guided the group to bring more people to God. Bringing women who had just found God or whom weren't quite there yet, an opportunity for fellowship and understanding that they might otherwise not have gotten. To bring them blessings through prayer and to share stories of tragedy and triumph. To show them about having a relationship with God, and how much power there is in that, to show them hope and how to fight back against Satan, against evil. To encourage and guide their learning all for the glory of God, no matter the obstacles along the way. Satan is cunning don't forget. I'd hate to think of all the ways they got attacked spiritually, even attempting to help people find God, the words I got in that first meeting war war war weren't just meant for me.

The group had begun, after my initial deliverance from depression experience had already occurred. After I was already on the deliverance learning path, learning as much about evil as I did about God, they told me focus on God not evil, but God kept telling me war, and know thy enemy is an important war tactic! I wanted to know everything! I wanted to be able to fight back. I desperately wanted to keep this peace of mind I had found for the first time in my life, this Godly joy Satan was trying to steal.

I didn't attend the group weekly, more once or twice a month from memory, life got in the way, even after getting off the antidepressants I was still quite unwell, and didn't have any answers for why. I was just dragging myself from one day to the next. I was losing weight without trying, my joints would ache, and I was so fatigued. I probably should have kept going back to the doctor, trying to get more answers, but I was bitter about the antidepressants being the poison that had made me sick for so long, and that it had been missed by so many doctors and specialists. I felt I had suffered needlessly. I had also completely stopped drinking thanks to Gods blessings, an evening wine had become a crutch and a sleep aid, but now I had stopped the antidepressants I was sleeping much better and the nightmares that had been happening for so long, I also got a break from. Wine was no longer a needed crutch, it made sense this was the reason for weight loss, and I figured the exhaustion was my body just needing to heal, needing to rest, learning about God became a priority. I chatted to Him all day long in my head, watching a huge amount online and slowly the puzzle was coming together.

My relationship with God was growing exponentially. I knew the feeling of Jesus's love, and was trying to figure out how that worked and how I could keep that feeling. Especially as I was learning more about Satan, and how determined he would be to take that feeling away, as my relationship with God grew the attacks would get worse.

Meeting the ladies for coffee and fellowship slowly became something I looked forward to. I pushed myself to go, after years not leaving the house, it did me good. I got to hear some great stories and have friendships with women who didn't just want to be my friend because of horses, because I was a horse trainer and that was something they aspired to, be my friend because they wanted something from me, as had so often been the case when it came to horse women, even though half the women in the group were horse women!

This group of women the hope hub was definitely a gift from God, to show me I needed fellowship. Another thing God would use to transform me, and all credit to Him. Another stepping stone on the narrow path, and a source of prayer and support I was very much going to need going into 2023. My hardest year to date.

Lessons Learnt...

LESSON H

Needing others in fellowship

> "We who had sweet fellowship together walked in the house of God in the throng." Psalms 55:14 NASB (1995)

I've always been quite independent, as I've grown up, I've learnt not to need others. I tend to isolate rather than ask for help, especially when I was struggling with depression, anxiety and its related shame. I did not want to be a burden on others.

This is not Gods way; this is not horses' way either. Horses are herd animals and very much need each other, they are highly sociable creatures, living in quite large groups in the wild. Never alone, when kept alone by humans some become very distressed and anxious, it's all too much, they need their friends for support, comfort and safety.

I've learnt I really do need the same, all the fellowship I have found since finding God has been amazing. It allows my journey to continue much faster, it provides me like the horses' comfort, support and safety, and a lot of wisdom from others. Amen, thankyou God for bringing all these amazing people into my life. May my fellowship continue to grow with my wisdom and love for God.

LESSON I

Horses know our hearts

> "Would not God find this out? For He knows
> the secrets of the heart." Psalms 44:21 NASB

God knows us better than we know ourselves, he knows our true hearts. Who we are deep down at soul level, there is no hiding anything, we cannot trick God, we need to be honest with ourselves.

This lesson very much applies to horses, the more time you spend with horses the more you realise the same is true. They see through us, they see when we are having a bad day, or are in a bad mood before we do. They hold a mirror up in front of us so we can see our true selves, some people like what they see, others do not, but it provides us the chance to become better, if we so choose.

Chapter 7

2023 TRAGIC REVELATIONS

It was now coming to the start of 2023.

I was saved, but I still didn't understand why I continued to be so unwell. I had found fellowship with other women. My mental health was the best it had been in years, being free of depression and anxiety was a revelation. My relationship with God was continuing to grow, my faith was built on stone and was unshakeable.

I also had three "knowings" floating around in my head that I of course didn't understand. The first was a car accident, all I knew is that I would be driving, look over my left shoulder, see a white car and have an accident. It was like a 1 or 2 sec vid I could play in my head, but by now I also knew that these "knowings" never ended well. So I was quite vocal about this one, for months I'd been talking about it, trying to prevent or subvert what ever was going to happen, like I had ever been able to that before!

It would come to pass in next few weeks.

The 2nd "knowing" had come to me mid 2022, it is me standing behind a woman while she speaks to a group of people standing in a paddock, this one still hasn't come to pass.

For over a year I thought it was something to do with horses, and so would try to follow a path I thought led there. Why I did this I'm not sure, you would think by now I would have learnt to run the other way! That I should know that it spelt a big change, usually a tragic event like death or fire, nope apparently, I like to forget this bit. I still remain clueless, with blind hope it's a good thing, especially now I had God on my side.

The 3rd "knowing" was the oldest, if I had to guess I'd say 20 years it had been in my mind. It was a place I'd named "the end of the world property". I had no idea how I would get there or where it was, but turned it out in the next 6mnths I would drive in the front gate, but for now I had another mountain to climb.

Although Mum and I were never close, she was still very much a big part of my life. She adored my children, more than she had ever adored myself. Verbalising she had never understood the attraction of having children, til she had grandchildren, she saw them fortnightly most of their lives and spoilt them rotten. Every time she had them it was like Christmas and much to my horror bought them endless toys. During the time I had very much stopped leaving the house, she would come pick them up Saturday, and bring them home the following day, they adored her as much as she them.

It was during covid and all the lockdowns that her health first took a turn, and after many tests was discovered first, she had a form of blood cancer which effected the plasma then later in 2021 that she also had Parkinson's disease. This changed everything as she was forced to give up the job in psychology, which she loved, followed by her ability to drive and she progressively declined. She lived in constant pain and her mobility diminished as time passed.

It was after the last lock down in the beginning of 2022, coming off the antidepressants, the worst of my stomach problems stopped, so I was less anxious about terrible cramps and needing the toilet immediately. Although still very unwell, we began to drive to visit her. I would go weekly with my kids staying fortnightly, and catching bus and train home the following day. They were 15 at this stage and still adored their grandmother, nanny as they called her. We watched her slow decline; she was only 76 and had still been working the year before as a psychologist. Happy to keep herself busy and her brain active.

It was Jan 2023 when tragedy struck, I was called by my brother to be told she had a fall. Breaking her pelvis in 8 places, with many other breaks in her spine. We rushed to the hospital the next day.

That was when it happened. When the knowing came to pass.

We had been to visit her. We went through the day, with my brother visiting at night. She was drugged to the eye balls for the pain and somewhat delirious. I'm not sure she knew we were there. Upon arrival they had been changing her bed, her screams of pain as they moved her were just heart breaking. Visiting hours were over and we had returned to the car. The car spaces were extremely tight, we had parked next to a low cement wall, I was tired and distressed at this turn of events with Mum. I told the kids be quiet I needed to concentrate, I looked over my left shoulder and tried to reverse out of the tight spot, the music was on and I didn't understand what had happened til the car was stuck. I had turned too sharply, the front left-hand bumper had hit the low wall, as I looked over my left shoulder, at the white 4wd waiting behind us.

It hit me all off a sudden, that bit where time slows down and everything lines up, the natural and the supernatural, the "knowing" had come to pass.

I knew at that moment, my mother would never leave that hospital, that her death was imminent. A wave of emotion and grief rocked me, I pulled myself together, moving the car off the wall and reversing out again, trying to comprehend.

The next 3mnths were a roller-coaster, her health went up and down. There were days like the first where she was out of it in pain, and others with hope where she seemed to be improving. But I just couldn't shake it, that moment of the accident. I just knew she wasn't leaving that hospital, despite talks of her going to rehabilitation. All through that time I would be hit with waves of grief. God preparing me. I'm not sure. I felt lost and confused. I was so very unwell myself still, just trying to survive, the 90 min each way drive we made 3 or 4 times a week, it all seemed very surreal.

I tried to encourage my aunts, her many sisters to come visit. I knew time was short, but they didn't know that, they waited intending to visit later when she was in rehab. I didn't know how to explain, that would be too late.

Those months at the time felt so long, there was so much pain and suffering for my mother, but looking back it feels like the blink of an eye. They eventually talked palliative care, her sisters rushed to her side, but it was mostly too late then. Too late to chat and say goodbye, so much pain, endless drugs were kinder. She was barely hanging on, to many complications too much pain, it was her time to go, she made her peace with God and said goodbye.

The "knowing" had come to pass again, in the most terrible way, but like dads passing I was well prepared. I couldn't explain it to anyone, who would believe me anyway. I knew she believed and had spoken to the Chaplin before it was too late, she was now with God, there's very much a peace in that, a relief.

Most of the big events like this I had walked in life, I had very much done alone, but this time I was very far from alone. God made sure I knew that, the fellowship ladies whom I had barely seen for months showed me what true fellowship was. Caring for those that need it, supporting each other, the flowers arrived, then the food. I was shocked, other friends did the same, sending condolences and so much food. I felt guilty, almost that people cared so much. It was foreign and very much a blessing, Dad's passing had been very different. Life was crushing me, but with all the support I stood strong. I knew she was in a better place with God. God made sure to use people so that I never felt alone, to remind me he was with me always.

I lent on God hard over the following weeks, tried to understand why these things were happening, the things I had learnt. I wondered what would happen next, just when you think things can't get worse, they do. But finally for the first time I picked up a Bible, and began to read, the next hurdle would come all too soon.

To tell a secret ...

I don't know if is it right to include this part of my story, or if it is better left unsaid, but it made me whom I became. It was the beginning of evil in my life, maybe it explains why things in my life happened the way they did. Why life had had so many hurdles, so much evil from such a young age. Was Satan trying to break me, maybe Satan knew my story would bring others to God. Does God have plans for me that I can't even comprehend yet. That Satan has been trying to stop, it would definitely be my greatest lesson in forgiveness.

I ask myself the questions, does evil happen so young to open doors to allow access? To give a foothold? Was this why my brain had been so broken? Was this why spirits of depression and anxiety were able to get their claws in so young? Through shame and fear? Would telling this secret explain so much? Help another find freedom? Help another understand their own hurdles in life? Their own tragedies? Why they are the way they are? Would it break the power and shame walked for so long, evict the fear that had brought the nightmares?

My whole life I never told anyone. I always protected her. I didn't want her to be hurt, she was my mother, but now she is gone.

The final shock of finding out the truth was greater than the secret, it should never have been this way. It was never my fault, it was never her fault, it was a shame that should never have existed, a secret that should never have been kept.

I always thought Mum didn't know, so I didn't tell. But in those final days I found out she knew, had known all along, maybe she thought I would forget, had forgotten.

In those final few days as she lay in the bed asleep, the drugs keeping her free from pain in the moment, sleep a blessing. Two of her sisters sat there as well, the weight of the room heavy. I asked a question, "I wonder what heaven is like?" In unison, they both spoke at once, words that took me back nearly 40 years, words spoken by my mother back then, words that would have a devastating impact on my life. "SSSHHHHHHHHHH WE DON'T TALK ABOUT IT!"

It was like being punched, the understanding those words brought, those words years before spoken by my mother. Knowing she had known all along, taking away my belief she didn't know, had never known. I had protected her all these years for nothing, thinking it would hurt her, that this had happened under her nose, not wanting to make her life harder than I believed I already had. The emotion welled up and spurted out, confusion, anger, tears, betrayal, devastation.

Who was this woman dieing in the bed? She was a person I had never known, not the wonderful mother everyone told me I had. Letting everyone think there was something wrong with me. Telling everyone that I was difficult, a horrible baby, how she never slept for caring for me, that I never slept through a night til I was 8 years old. That she didn't understand what was wrong with me, my panic attacks and out bursts of anger making her life so hard, her finding sympathy from others. I heard it over and over again as a child, her complaints about me, she was ashamed of me, I was a chore. When she knew all along what had broken me, why I was the way I was. The way evil had come and stolen my sanity, my innocence. Why I struggled with life. But I wasn't difficult I was damaged, broken, scared, but she made sure nobody knew. I grew ashamed of making her life hard, guilty of being so difficult.

The memory is so strong it could be yesterday.

This is one incident, how many other times it had happened I will never know, my age when it started, I'm not 100% sure. 3 or 4 maybe younger, she was older in her early teens, lived across the road, was there to baby sit, distract me, give Mum a break, peace. A tent fortress she had made, so if the door was opened, we were hidden, my pants were off I lay on my back, without details I was poked and prodded, then my turn to do to her. I must have known it was wrong. l must have wanted this game to stop, it hurt, she screamed, loudly.

The kitchen was metres away, Mum would have burst in the door after that scream and seen, understood.

"SHHHHHH DONT TELL ANYONE" that's what Mum said, perhaps hoping I would forget, I probably did forget for a time, but in my late teens I remembered. But I thought she didn't know, my mother always seemed so fragile, crying or on the verge of anger and yelling, we walked on egg shells. I didn't want to make it worse, so I didn't tell anyone. I didn't want her to feel bad, that she couldn't protect me. But I was wrong, she did know, she should have tried to help me. I was just a little girl, instead I was made to feel ashamed, to be told I was difficult for being the way I became, for making her life hard.

The realisation was a huge shock. I didn't explain to my aunts. I walked out that day, from her hospital room. I was devastated. I didn't return, she passed a few days later. I let her die thinking I had forgotten. I let her have that peace, was this an easy thing to do, no, but for once I was allowed to be free of that lie. To escape the guilt and shame of being the difficult child that had made her life so very hard, to break the curse spoken over me.

I now understand this incident opened the door for evil to torment me for the next 40years, the evil attacks of guilt and shame relentless, til I finally found safety and protection of God.

I still debate if it is right to include this story, even though it played a big part in the making of my life. If Mum was still alive, I would never persecute her, have her feel that same shame.

God says we must love but more importantly we must forgive. I lived a life of guilt and shame for making her life so hard, being so difficult, it triggered and brought on anxiety and depression, but neither guilt nor shame are of God, nor are secrets.

As hard as it is, I have forgiven her. I let the fire refine me. I didn't let myself turn to bitterness, which only leads to anger, she was gone now, there was nothing left to say. I needed to forgive, to forget the past in order to be free to be at peace.

I have cast this shame and guilt out of my life, destroyed this lie. I would not let it return. If God can use me sharing this experience for good, to bring one more person to Him, to help them understand why they are the way they are, to help them walk the narrow path, to save another soul, to break another person free. Then so let it be done, may suffering become good in the name of Jesus. May I always walk in peace and joy.

Lessons Learnt...

LESSON J

Real healing comes from the root.

> "See to it that no one fails to obtain the grace of God; that no 'root of bitterness' springs up and causes trouble, and by it many become defiled." Hebrews 12:15 ESV

God grants us the blessing of healing many things in our lives, many of these require you to get to the root of the problem. To remove the root of evil, the root of bitterness, this can require some deep digging on our own part, to be able to remove this root. We may need to dig into the past to be able to finally put it behind us, forgive, to finally be able to find healing and move on, we then find a new way of being, a new peace and joy.

    Horses are much the same, we must get to the root of the problem, achieve real training, start from the beginning, go through all the basics to find the root of the problem. Once we have found the root of the problem, we can help the horse heal. Help the horse have a new understanding, remove the root of the problem for a better future, so the horse will understand a new way of being. Free from the past, have their own peace and joy, a safe future.

LESSON K

Forgiveness and empathy

> "Be kind to one another, tender-hearted, forgiving one another, as God in Christ forgave you." Ephesians 4:32 ESV

Forgiveness is by far the most important lesson we will ever learn in our lives. Horses have taught me empathy and reinforced the importance of kindness, but it cannot compare to the lessons I am still learning everyday which come from God. He forgives our every sin and has empathy for us beyond which I can comprehend. I bow down to you oh Lord, I thank you beyond measure for sending us your son Jesus, to die for our sins, our salvation. Please forgive me for everything I have done which is not of you Lord. I repent of my sins and forgive all those that have ever hurt me, thankyou praise Jesus.

Chapter 8

THE ONE WORD YOU NEVER WANT TO HEAR. CANCER

It was now march 2023, Mum had just passed. I was completely surrendered to God. I just wanted His will in my life. I was slowly learning to pray, and would collect prayers I found online, slowly getting into the habit of reading ones that touched me at the beginning of each day. I had also committed to reading the Bible. I didn't know where to start, so thought I would start at the beginning, read it like a book til I understood more how to use the power of the word in my life.

I had now been blessed with deliverance from so much. I really felt saved, reborn, my mind was in a continual process of renewal, the learning was endless. I started to move from less focus on evil and how it worked, to more focus of fighting back. I had learnt a lot about how my choices in life had allowed the enemy to do so much damage. Although I knew Jesus had won the war for us. It didn't feel like that, I felt I was under attack, riding an emotional roller-coaster. Feeling the amazing peace and joy of Jesus love, then a short time later being engulfed again in the flesh, feeling down and heavy. My brain stumbling into the negative, although I had learnt God had armour, we could wear to protect ourselves, actually wearing it takes a lot more understanding, a lot more wisdom. I prayed daily for the wisdom, I needed for God to show me the way, provide wisdom and understanding.

Mums passing was still very surreal, it's like you know they are gone but they don't feel gone, she had been such a big part of our lives especially my kids, her passing left a big hole in our daily lives, but God was very much there to fill that hole for me. I'm not sure I would have coped so well otherwise.

Forgiveness is a huge part of the God journey, so I very much chose not to dwell on the past, not let myself go over it in my brain. Doing my best to capture and evict those thoughts as they appeared, not become angry or resentful, to stop bitterness taking over. To also not be over whelmed with sadness and grief, these emotions were just waiting for a crack in my armour to take hold and bring me down, to distract and divert me. Forgiveness is a journey, and not an easy one. Evil will use the smallest thought or incident from the past, place it in your mind and then build on in til it starts to take over, til it then connects with emotion that is not from God. Satan then uses that to trigger you, to cause you to have an angry outburst, or become offended by someone that had nothing to do with that original memory. All of a sudden you find yourself living in Satan's world not Gods, you get tricked, it takes some practice to recognise it before you take that wrong path, this is why the path is narrow. Getting side tracked happens without you realising it, so very easily, like with horses you eat a lot of dirt as you fall off the path!

The Hope Hub ladies were also very supportive, and I have no doubt their prayers were working. The weekly fellowship was something I very much looked forward to, especially now I had more time, not driving across Sydney to the hospital multiple times a week. I made friends with women without us talking about horses, though that was still a topic that regularly came up, my interest was wanning, I didn't want to talk horses. I wanted to know more about God, hear people's testimonies, about people's lives, about how and when God had stepped in. I was also fascinated about their children loving God, turning to God, and wondered if I could bring my own kids to do the same, for them to grow up like I never had, with a greater understanding of the world, with a life manual of how they should be treated, and how to treat others, of understanding they didn't need to worry about anything that the future brought. That they just needed a relationship with God and they would be led.

These ladies would also prove a great support when the disaster stuck that would shake me to my core. Physically I looked terrible, I had now lost 20kgs without trying, but had just tried to ignore it. Especially with everything that had been going on with Mum. It was easier just to ignore. I figured it was due to stopping the antidepressants, never drinking wine, at first it was great, all the weight I had slowly put on over 10 years disappeared. But problem was the weight loss didn't stop, my clothes had started to fall off me, ribs protruded, plus I was terribly tired all the time, feeling like I could sleep for a week. I was dragging myself through every day. I wanted to go back to work with the horses now my mental health was better, my savings were running out. I tried to find a way to live like this. I was still angry at doctors for missing the side effects for so long, I didn't really have anyone to talk to especially being a single parent. When I brought up my concern with friends, they often would say how lucky I was to be losing weight so easily. I just wanted my life back. I just turned totally to God and got through one day at a time, figuring he had a plan for me. I just needed to watch for the signs to follow, have faith.

Now Mum was gone I had no excuse. I reluctantly dragged myself off to the doctor. My doctor is not the most empathic person I have ever met, I was considering changing doctors after suggestions from friends, but thought I would go back one last time. Upon hoping on the scales, we were both a bit shocked at the number. I was easily 15kg under where I should be, not good.

Being a cigarette smoker, which I know she hated, fair enough, she immediately sent me off for CT scan on my chest. A message was received to my phone asking me to return to doctor for the results less than 48hours later. I made the appointment to be told the CT had found masses on both my lungs and thyroid, not good. When your doctor who lacks empathy starts to look worried, then that definitely starts alarm bells ringing. She arranged a referral to a lung specialist at local hospital and a thyroid biopsy, as well as numerous blood tests.

The lung specialist was a few weeks wait. The thyroid biopsy the following week. After the thyroid biopsy again, I was messaged to return to doctor. Upon entering the office and watching her read over the results, I swear she went a shade or 2 paler. She then slid the sheet of paper across the desk, of the two masses found in my thyroid, one had come back with the words you never want to read on any results: Papillary thyroid cancer.

Oh no. I nearly fell off the chair. I wasn't expecting that at all. No wonder she looked grey. Cancer is the last word you ever want to hear, there was definitely not a knowing about this.

The doctor actually made a mistake on what to do next, but it turned out for the best, a move of God I would say, as things played out. She told me I needed to see an endocrine surgeon, but that (the mistake) I needed to wait til I had the results for my lungs, to wait til after I had seen the lung specialist, it would end up being months before I saw the endocrine surgeon.

So, I went home and did as you do, I googled! You always find the best and the worst online, but upon findings a couple of support groups their stories were much more helpful. It was slow growing and not terminal. Among friends outside Hope Hub, I ended up joining what was starting to feel like a club, a club you never wanted to join, with 3 others going through their own or partners cancer journey at the same time, it was very surreal.

The weeks leading up to the lung specialist passed quickly, there was nothing I could do but wait. Though there was also some relief in knowing that everything that had been going on wasn't just in my head, that at least I was finally getting some answers. I did the best I could not too over think it, and again put all my trust in God. It was one heck of a test of faith. I think in these moments people go one of two ways. They get angry at God, take up the why me train of thought, what have I done, I don't to deserve this, how could God let this happen, self-pity. The other train of thought is the, help me God, I need you more than ever, and lean into God harder surrender more. This is our free choice. I chose to turn to God more, to read the Bible more, to edit my thoughts more, to get to know God more. To make my foundation in God set in stone, so that whatever would come next, I wouldn't be moved.

Was this easy, absolutely not. Satan wants you to be scared, angry, hurt, desperate, depressed, anxious. He tries everything to make you walk these paths, to push you off God's path the path of peace and joy. Did I take the wrong path more than once, absolutely, but I was still learning to turn to the Bible, to read even when I didn't understand, to sleep with Bible playing, to call out these evil spirits and tell them no, I was learning all the ways I could feed my spirit man to feed my soul, to become stronger in God. I was still learning, my armour was still weak, but I just needed to live one day at a time, the future I gave to God.

The appointment with the lung specialist finally arrived, he is a nice man, made me feel comfortable, but looked very concerned at the CT results. None of this was good, a lung function test and a PET scan were ordered. What's a PET scan, basically, a PET scan is what they use to look for cancer, they inject you with radiation and put you in the machine. It's only available in the largest hospitals, and is very specialised and expensive, the radiation symbols on the heavy metal doors, and the technician having to be behind a wall so they are not exposed doesn't bring much hope, it's a place you don't want to be.

After these tests I got a phone call, and my follow up appointment with the lung specialist was brought forward. I figured at least I didn't have long to wait. Not realising this was in fact a huge alarm bell! Upon arrival at the appointment, it took a while for the specialist to load results, the hospital system in the computer didn't want to load.

Then he got that same look my doctor did, the pale look the bad news look. The results of the lung function test weren't good, and the results of the PET scan had come back that there is heat in that area, showing abnormal grow of cells, at least I think that's what he said. It was the next few words that I remember clearly, where time seems to slow down, much like falling off a horse your mind tries to compute what is happening, brace for impact. If I was a computer the loading circle would have slowed right down, then he said it,

Lung cancer, Lymphoma or sarcoidosis. Oh no, that's really not good.

Dad had died of lung cancer and Mum of a blood related cancer only just recently, what are the odds those were two types that were spoken, I felt sick.

He then picked up the phone, within a matter of minutes I was having another referral shoved in my hand, an appointment had been made with the Lung surgeon this time. He had an available appointment that day in

30mins. Oh dear, it was all very surreal how fast things started to happen. Your emotions sway to and fro, you feel very off-balance. I jumped in the car to surgeons' office just down the road, he looked at the results, then booked me in for a Lung biopsy the following week at one of the major Sydney hospitals. No time to waste.

I didn't realise at the time like I do now. How worried I should have been at this urgency, the hospital system especially when you are using the public system is slow, there are usually substantial wait times. When they are rushing you through, it's because they consider it an emergency. Your life can literally be on the line, the sooner they have answers and treatment can begin the better your chances. Ignorance was bliss in my case. I just did what I was told, trusted that God had my back, it was another week or so before it would really hit me.

A Lung biopsy involves them sticking tubes down your throat, into your lungs in order to collect a tissues sample. Therefore, unlike the thyroid biopsy, you are under a full anaesthetic, completely knocked out. It's quite disconcerting, dressed in a gown in hospital ward in a bed waiting. I was last for the day and they were running late, it wasn't a good time, the future was very unknown, talking to other patients in those situations also isn't a great idea. The man in the bed next to me started a conversation. Telling me more than a few horror stories about his own journey, how he was now missing half a lung and what some of the treatments had done to his health. It's a blessing the Bible teaches to edit and capture our thoughts, because mine were ready to be like a horse that tries to bolt, ready at any moment to be totally out if control, but I managed to keep control, keep my mind from bolting.

There were a few moments, when I was with the Hope Hub ladies when I realised, I couldn't even talk about it without that bolting horse dragging me across the road! I would be chatting and be asked if I was OK, or what the doctors were saying, did I know what was wrong, and the emotions would run right over the top of me. The tears would burst out and catch me off guard. I didn't realise how close I was to breaking. How evil was just sitting there waiting for its chance to jump in, to let that horse run clear over the top of me, drag me down the street and around the block!

There a saying I'd read on a coffee mug as a child which I never completely understood it reads: "I think. Therefore, I am ..."

It was at this time in my life it fully dawned on me, and I understood why the Bible said to capture every thought. I realised speaking the words, repeating what doctors were telling me, even though they weren't truth yet, gave those words power, gave them a truth I didn't want them to have. I didn't fully understand word curses at that point, how we speak things over ourselves, even saying I feel sick or I feel tired or I feel anxious, we make them real. We give evil a foothold when we believe those words, and it becomes real. But I was quickly learning, a wisdom I'd come to learn about much more in the following weeks, as I learnt to wear the armour of God, the belt of truth, and how to declare and dedicate myself to God, with the sword of the word.

I'd been given an appointment to see the lung specialist again during my last appointment, it had been set for 6 weeks later, as a standard protocol. Which allowed time for tests to be done, along with the lung biopsy, I was sent for more CT scans. Previously, after the PET scan I had received a call to bring the appointment forward, this time that did not happen, I would need to wait what was just over 4 weeks to get the results.

It was during these 4 weeks God would again step in and change my life, provide wisdom I never knew existed, that would provide blessing like I didn't know existed. God had my back.

If you had asked me what Revival was, I would have been totally clueless! So, when I was invited to a tent revival, I happily agreed to go, with all the stress of the unknown and endless tests I wanted more God in my life, and perhaps this was a way. A friend around the corner from me was keen, so we convinced our teenage kids to join us and off we went.

A huge white tent has been set up at the horse trotting track, that had to be a good sign, a huge stage constructed at the front and hundreds of chairs in rows. I had definitely never been to anything like this before, this was as far from my catholic upbringing as you could get!

The first half an hour was music, a band and everyone singing. I didn't yet understand worship music like I do now. It was foreign to my ears, songs I had never heard before, everybody singing along. The words displayed on a screen. I wondered why they performed. I wondered what was the point. I just wanted to sit down and hear them speak. Tim Hall was the pastor, this was his ministry, another pastor provided the tent, there were a few different churches who had come together to hold this event. Considering this was only 6 months ago, to my now writing this testimony, I'm amazed how far I've come and how much I've learnt. I certainly didn't know then what I would come to know now, and it's exciting to know that in a further 6 - 12 months I'll probably look back to my writing this and be amazed, at how little I still knew and how much more I would come learn.

I don't remember what Tim Hall spoke about that day, what his message was about. I do remember, after his speaking for about an hour, he called people up the front who wanted to give their life to God. I felt I had already given my life to God, but cautiously made my way to the front regardless.

I'd seen it on TV before and was very sceptical. Watching him make his way along the rows of people, touching some, not touching others, but most people went down. Some so they were lying flat out others sitting, a seemingly dazed look on their face. I wasn't sure what it was all about it be honest. When it came to my turn and he looked in my eyes and said a few words, which I now can't remember, it was again like that time slowing feeling. Where your rational mind fights reality, in reality I looked down to see myself tipping over, he hadn't pushed me, he had barely touched me. But saw my feet tip back on my heels and a came to be sitting on the floor. Wondering if I'd done that myself, made a choice or if some higher power had in fact touched me.

My rational brain fought my spirit to understand exactly what had happened. Upon returning to my seat, the teenagers were all asking to leave, this seemed fair, we had been there more than a couple of hours which they hadn't been prepared for, but hadn't complained, so we made our way home. I was left with a lot to ponder.

The same tent revival was also scheduled for the following night. I was in two minds whether to go, physically I was really tired and not up to driving myself the hour at night, so when a different friend called from Hope Hub and said she will be there in 20mins to pick me up, I quickly raced to get organised, not letting my brain or body talk me out of going.

This night was to be very different, since God delivered me from depression, I now had a much greater understanding and very much a belief in deliverance and healing. I understood that when Jesus died on the cross His gift to the world was an inheritance of deliverance and healing. I was only just fully understanding how big this gift was, and just how much could be achieved with faith and belief. That not only did the devil attack our minds, but our physical health as well.

My mind has already been freed of so much, my faith was strong, but little did I know I was going to be blessed much further, my faith growing much bigger.

The night progressed much the same as the night before, except I had arrived with 2 of the ladies from the Hope Hub. Pam and Leigh, worship began, then the message, again I don't remember anything that Tim Hall spoke of that night.

The next bit I remember as clear as yesterday. I was standing with Pam, Leigh came and grabbed me, knowing my health issues she marched me over to a woman named Josie. As soon as Leigh said this is the lady with cancer, Josie jumped right in, not speaking to me but to the demon in me, the demon of death. I didn't even know there was a demon called death. I felt myself smile, not my own smile, but something else, something wicked. My lips curling in a grimace, I couldn't get it off my face, it felt unnatural. Josie continued to speak, to call it out, looking me straight in the eye, not looking at me, looking at the evil, at the demon, then I went down, flat on my back this time. I could hear Josie clearly, calling out the demon telling it too leave. Speaking her own testimony of being healed of brain cancer at the same time. I understood her words I believed them. I forced my own mouth to speak the same, out, out, out. I knew I believed; I had total faith. It was again a moment where your own brain is watching something happen, trying to comprehend, my body twitched, convulsed even on the floor. It was very strange, my brain not quite understanding why it did not have control of what was going on in my body. Wondering if I was doing this or something apart from me. Satan was still trying to trick me; the evil had a strong hold of me.

Then I felt it, a burn in my chest, deep inside me. A burning heat right at the spot where the doctors had told me the cancer was, stronger and stronger the burning became, and then as she commanded death to leave, used the authority Jesus has blessed her with, that burn started to move, up towards my throat, I felt it rise slowly, slowly towards my mouth. I started coughing as it finally was forced up out of me, my brain registering the truth of what happened. Fully grasping the understanding that death had been evicted, yay praise Jesus. My mind then clamped onto the fact, the revelation as an absolute, I was healed. I said thankyou and Josie left moving onto the next person whom needed Gods help. I must have sat there for a good 10mins, letting it sink in, feeling a lightness as the weight of death was lifted.

It was about a week later; I saw a video of Josie's own testimony. First surviving breast cancer with a guiding hand from God 12 years earlier, after being given a death sentence by doctors. Then more recently, months in fact, surviving brain cancer after being delivered by Kathryn Krick online. Josie was quite literally told by the doctors she was a medical miracle, the stage 4 cancer gone, amazing and very exciting. I had more faith than ever that I had been delivered from death, that when I returned to the specialist, I would be told that I did not in fact have either lung cancer or lymphoma.

Over those next couple of weeks. I kept my faith strong, in my mind I held onto it as truth. I would not be swayed. When the day finally came to see the specialist, I was definitely nervous and as will often happen in these situations, evil had one last go and he was running an hour late. I said the 'our father' over and over in my head, while I sat waiting, alone with God, I sat in the cold hard plastic chair, finally my name was called.

The lung specialist greeted me and started bring up my files, instead of the paler look I'd seen the doctors get so often on their faces he got a look of confusion, he brought up more images on the computer screen, read the report over. I held my breath; this is what it must be like to sit in court waiting to hear the verdict. "All clear" he said, your results have come back good, everything normal, the look of confusion still on his face "maybe because you're so tall?" Wait what? I wanted to burst out laughing in joy. I was in shock, this time a good shock, like winning lotto. Relief washed over me. No lung cancer. No lymphoma. Not even sarcoidosis. Hooray praise Jesus! He wrote me another CT referral, told me to get it done in 12 months' time, he will see me then. He seemed more shocked than I did, but then I knew the truth, I knew the miracle I had been blessed with.

The weight of worry I didn't even know I was carrying was lifted. God is so good, my faith grew stronger in that moment, just when you think you can't have more faith it grows yet again. I left the hospital that day and raced home to share the good news. I must have thanked God a thousand times over. I knew non-Christians wouldn't understand, would think that I just got lucky. But I knew the truth. I felt that evil rise up out of my chest and leave me that day at revival, and now I knew God would also help me through the rest.

Now it was time to deal with the thyroid results, the papillary cancer they told me I had. An appointment was made with the endocrine surgeon. I desperately at worst, only wanted half my thyroid removed. As 2 masses had been discovered on the right side, only one of these a high risk for cancer, the idea that I would need to be on medication for the rest of my life was horrifying. After dealing with side effects from antidepressants, I did not want to walk that path. I prayed for answers. I prayed for God to show me the way. I just wanted to finally be well. I prayed healing prayers daily.

Again, the specialist was very nice, they had got me into an appointment with only a 2 week wait. During the appointment he did another ultrasound in his office, found another mass, a 3rd one that had been missed, this time on the left side. I was also told that although the 2nd mass on the right had biopsied clear, he didn't like the look of it, it also looked suspicious. He wanted to remove my whole thyroid. I must have gone green, so not just half I asked? Any chance of just half, he looked me in the eye and said "we will send you for more biopsy's ", this time at a place that specialises, who does theses all day long and will get a more reliable result. Excellent, exactly what I needed, more time for more tests to come back negative.

This biopsy was quite different, the original one was awful. Your thyroid is so close to your face, you can see and feel them slowly poking around taking the sample, it seems to take forever. At this new place the technician was like a ninja, crazy fast, he had a team working with him, to ensure the sample was what was needed to get a guaranteed result.

It was about a 2-week period between specialist appointments, to allow time for the biopsy and results. During this time God again showed me what I needed to do. I stumbled again across a video of Josie. Whom God had used to deliver me from death, latest testimony. She was testifying about her recent breast reconstruction, about how she declared to the Lord exactly how it was going to go, thanking Him as if it had already happened. Right down to the surgery being practically pain free, zero complications, even that her hospital room would be private and have a view. Testifying that when the time came for the surgery, that was exactly what happened. Right down to the private room and the view! Wow I thought that's amazing. I'll just do that then. I'll declare exactly what is going to happen when I go back to the thyroid specialist. I have to look back and laugh at myself, the Bible says to have childlike faith, and that was absolutely what I was walking in. My love and faith in Jesus were immense. I didn't tell anyone, so I didn't have anyone put any doubt in me. After the other cancer results came back as they did, and Josie again appearing with the answer I needed, I jumped right in, zero doubt.

From that day until my next appointment, I declared. I declared in the name of Jesus, that I would walk into the office and be told all the new results were benign. I declared I would be told that I needed only half my thyroid removed. I declared I would be told I wouldn't need the follow up radioactive iodine treatment, I declared I would be told I wouldn't need to be on medication every day for the rest of my life. In the name of Jesus. Praise Jesus, thank you.

Every single day I declared it. I believed it. I had full faith that like the Bible says, you believe it is done and it is done. Praise Jesus.

And you know what, that's exactly what happened. I walked into that office, after the specialist was running late, of course, Satan will use any and every chance to sow doubt. I sat down and I waited. I watched him read the results; I watched that same look of confusion come over his face as the lung specialist. I heard him say those exact words I had declared. Biopsy shows benign; only need to remove half, no radioactive iodine; no medication daily for the rest of my life. Whoop whoop I cracked the biggest smile, praise Jesus I actually spoke this time. I wanted to laugh. I was filled with joy, the specialist spent the next half an hour explaining what would happen next, about the surgery I would need the risks etc. I could barely focus. I was so excited I wanted out of there, all worry had left me, whatever would happen next, I didn't need to worry. I knew God had my back. I knew I would get well. I just needed to believe, thank you Jesus!

As I sit here writing this now a couple of months has passed. I'm still waiting for surgery. I am under the public system, so they will only rush if there's a risk to my life or if the cancer will spread quickly. Neither of these are the case. I'm happy to wait. I now declare daily in Jesus name that the surgery will be easy, no complications, that I will have little pain, an easy recovery, that every cancer cell will be removed from my body, that I will get well, in Jesus' name. I declare that I know God has me, and I thank Jesus for His gift. I thank God for the blessings that have already been rained down on me.

Even without the surgery my health has been improving, my mind is constantly in renewal. I have put on weight and people keep telling me how much better I look, all glory to God to Jesus, but my story doesn't end here.

Once I understood how this legal system of heaven and earth worked, I was onto it! I never in my wildest dreams thought it worked like this. I never understood just how good God is. I pray every day for more wisdom and God is providing in abundance.

But in saying that Satan is a good lawyer himself, and as much as God blessed me, he got more and more pissed off! Even writing this testimony he hates, a lot. So, he keeps coming, tries other schemes, tries to get a foothold in other ways, finds other doors that I have left open. But I've lived so long with no way to fight back, no way to protect myself, so long in oppression, there was no way I was going to back down. He's not going to beat me, I keep pushing forward, find that knowledge, find the keys, discover the wisdom that God has provided. Jesus has won the war, and I was on His side, there was no stopping me now. I would keep getting back on the horse! Celebrate victory in God always.

Lessons Learnt...

LESSON L

Learning is hard don't give up

> "But as for You, be strong and do not give up, for your time work will be rewarded." 2 Chronicles 15:7 NIV

The journey to a relationship with God is hard, the path narrow. Spiritually we get attacked many times, physically things may also go awry. Sometimes it feels like there is little progress, sometimes it feels like we are going backwards. We feel exhausted and beaten up, but we must keep going. Breakthrough will come, the worse the journey, the better we will feel when get through the hard parts. When we learn the hard way, we don't forget the lesson, our faith grows. God has our back, he is watching. Stay steady on the narrow path, don't divert when it gets hard, don't get frustrated, never give up.

Horses very much involve learning the hard way, they are big strong animals, when things go wrong and we hit the ground. It is not much fun, we often feel a bit defeated and exhausted, but not giving up is extremely important. We must keep going, dust ourselves off, a breakthrough will come. We must commit to learning, to being better and keep going. Keep looking for an answer, a key to help them, something maybe you have missed, a hole in training, getting frustrated won't fix it. The end result is always worth it, you often are saving the horses future, its life, and securing a better one. Much like God does for us when we don't give up, when we keep battling towards achieving a relationship with Him. 100% worth it.

LESSON M

Don't use physical strength. Develop mental strength

> "God is our refuge and strength, a very present help in trouble." Psalm 41:1 ESV

We can't fight spiritual war with physical strength. When we get spiritually attacked no amount of physical fitness or training can help, things will go wrong, we get attacked, fear, anxiety, depression, frustrations will try to overtake us. We need mental strength to overcome this, we need courage to keep looking for the narrow path, to build our faith. We must stay strong in our belief of God, in faith, that he has a plan that is for the best. Negative emotions cause us to want to protect ourselves, to run away, or to lash out. But this is what the devil wants, how he wins the fights, but we must turn to God, give Him all our fear and worry. Develop our mental strengths through prayer and the word. Like getting physically fit, at first it is really hard. We must commit to getting better, over time and with practice, it gets much easier, comes more naturally. There becomes no more fear or anxiety about the spiritual attacks, we grow in our courage and confidence in the Lord, it becomes easier to keep the enemy at bay.

Training horses taught me alot of the same principles, we should never train a horse using physical strength, by force. We should be soft and use our brains, our mental strength, our intelligence. We must not let our own fear cause us to be rough, let us think this is the way to protect ourselves. To control the horse by force, or by fear. We must develop confidence by doing things the right way, having the horse trust us. By developing courage over time, develop our minds, things become easier with practice, come much more naturally. We gain experience, which lessens our fears, and we feel less and less the need to use physical strength or force. Our mental strength keeps us safe and on the right path like it does with God. Calm with no fear.

LESSON N

Learn what can go wrong. Be prepared.

> "Stay alert! Watch out for your great enemy the devil. He prowls around like a roaring lion, looking for someone to devour. Stand firm against him, and be strong in your faith." 1 Peter 5:8 NIV

A million things can go wrong training horses. The way to stay safe and best protect ourselves is to be prepared, be aware of what can go wrong and be cautious. Don't rush. Don't miss a step, this just allows an opportunity for yourself or the horse to be injured. The better prepared we are the more likely we are to see a problem before it happens, to prevent it.

An example being a horses first time wearing a saddle, we must go slow, watch for all signs of worry, do the girth up slowly, allow the horse to take a few steps before each adjustment. To get used to the feeling, to avoid problems before they happen, it's much fairer on the horse and safer for us.

If we just throw the saddle on and yank the girth tight with no preparation then the risk of the horse getting a fright is massively increased. The result of this fear being the horse runs, bucks and injures itself or me. Being prepared to know what may cause things to go wrong is very important. Being aware of the consequences of things going wrong is just as important, this is wisdom that keeps us safe. We must know the steps to take, to know the consequences of the mistakes made, to be prepared and take the steps needed to try and stop disaster from happening.

These are hard lessons learnt when things do go wrong, when you aren't alert, when you miss a step and the horse isn't prepared.

To achieve this in the kingdom of God. To be prepared means knowing the enemy, to have wisdom of and understand the tactics Satan will use for an attack against us. Which is guaranteed to happen. We must be alert of his schemes, how he will try to gain footholds, or use a door left open.

We must prepare ourselves, take the steps needed to stop these attacks. Repent and renounce, stop sinning the best we can, to not speak badly over ourselves or others, even in the simplest way. Calling myself a fool, or even tired, or a child annoying, can invite him in. Every word can open a door.

Like with horses, we must be prepared in order to keep ourselves safe. This requires much learning, like horses we must try to look ahead, to see things coming, to try and prevent disasters from happening, by altering our words and actions. We must not miss a step, Satan is smarter more practiced than us, but we have God on our side, so we just need to know how not to go wrong, not bring consequences upon ourselves, to not have the horse get a fright.

Chapter 9

TEETH AND CIGARETTES

In my previous chapter, I had just discovered the power of declaring. How powerfully God can move in our lives when we have childlike faith. How mind-blowing miracles can happen every day, too all of us. Not just in stories you hear about things that happen to other people. Therefore, I need to further testifying about how powerful declaration is, it's so much fun watching the medical profession get shocked by miracles. What I know is an act of God, leaves me in awe of God, this time it would be the dentist.

When you start to declare something, and thank God and Jesus for something that hasn't happened yet. It is very easy for Satan to whisper thoughts to your rational brain; about how irrational you are being. How in fact these things won't be happening, how your child like faith is in fact childish, that you are believing in fairy tales.

As I've since discovered, I'm far from the only one that let's nearly 20 years pass between dentist visits. Then when you do need to go, because there is something wrong in your mouth. You worry about all the other things that they will find, and how much it is going to cost you, so you end up just putting it off for longer and longer.

It was about 5 years ago when the mark first started appearing on my front tooth, yes you read that right front tooth! Front left and stupidly, because I can't word curse myself and call myself a damn fool! I left it, no doubt it was caused by my smoking, another thing I'd been doing for 20 years. But the idea of going to the dentist with all the stomach issues I had been having, seemed insurmountable. I just didn't think I could do it, didn't think I could bare it, so I left it, and left it, and left it. Until of course it got worse, and worse, and like rotten fruit sitting next to the other, it spread. First to my eye tooth on the left, then to my other front tooth. I was horrified, and it was getting so you could see it whenever I smiled and my top lip rose. I started to become very self-conscious, holding my mouth strangely so it didn't show. This also brought the thoughts to mind, if my front teeth are this bad, how bad are the rest of my teeth going to be, the ones I couldn't see! Eeek! I currently had no filings, but nearly 20 years had passed since anyone had looked, and I'd had suffered ulcers and gastritis for years. Literally coughing up bile daily, I figured all the acid could have done immense damage, especially when you could see how bad just the front were!

I'd only taken my kids to dentist a few months beforehand, after missing a few years and they both had cavities. So I dreaded to think about myself. All I could think of was horror stories you hear, about teeth needing to be pulled, or needing crowns, or even dentures, and then the cost. Australia is blessed with a good public health system but that does not include teeth. It was something I worried about a lot. Satan loved to keep me awake at night, imagining the worst. Fear.

But slowly I was learning just how much you needed to give your worry to God, this is actually one of my favourite things about my relationship with God. It's like I get to be a kid again, and not worry about things kids don't worry about. Where kids didn't have to worry about things like cooking dinner, electricity bills, car service, with God I got to do the same, but on an even bigger scale. I wasn't supposed to be worried about anything, my health, the bills, my kids even. I was literally supposed to dump it all in God's lap and have child life faith He would come up with plan, a better plan than I could ever come up with. Of course Satan tries to make us think otherwise, but I was learning more and more to edit my thoughts and keep totally turned towards God, no matter what the current worry was, Is this easy? Heck no! It takes so little for our train of thought to head of in the wrong direction, and when it's holes in your front teeth, there's a constant reminder every time you see your reflection. It was getting to stage my hand would go to cover my mouth every time I spoke, my smile distorting, shame creeping in.

So finally, after being blessed so mightily with my health results I gave this to God. Please God I need a solution to my teeth. I need a way to pay for them as well, so it began I figured I'd go for broke. "I declare in the name of Jesus, I will go to the dentist and the dentist will say 'you have no holes in any of your back teeth.' I declare in the name of Jesus that my front teeth will be an easy fix."

This was at the same time I was declaring my thyroid results, so I figured I was asking a lot, but being persistent is the key, the Bible tells us, practically nag God! Done! I certainly had nothing to lose, what's the worst that could happen.

Then the thyroid results came back. What a blessing, it certainly gave me renewed hope and persistence, so I kept it up. Trying not to worry, and when the worry came, I declared again, thanking God.

Then the first box got ticked, paying, I had just completed my tax return and surprisingly got back 2000 dollars. That was it, no excuse not to go anymore. I technically didn't have a dentist, but God wants us to notice the little things, and on Facebook I kept seeing a recommendation for a dental clinic on a parent's page. I'd rung the one up the road, they had a six week wait, so I tried this one they weren't far, next week they could fit me in, done! At least I would know exactly how bad things were, and how much it would cost.

The day arrived; I can't say I didn't dread it. I mean who looks forward to the dentist. I sat in the chair while he looked in my mouth and waited, praying the Our Father over and over in my head, then the moment, you wait for after declaring and thanking God for a certain outcome, will that be what is said? Will God bless me again, I held onto faith, the dentist spoke, "you haven't had any work done before ", "you have no cavities in any back teeth ", "you must have very hard enamel!" Woohooo go God!

What about the fronts I ask? "Oh, those holes are just minor ", "it's just cosmetic, because they are in the front that makes them look bad, not to worry easy fix ". I could have melted off the chair in relief, praise Jesus, thank you, thank you, thank you God.

But he says, you have minor periodontal disease, we will need to fully go over each tooth, by this stage minor was a word I wasn't slightest bit worried to hear! He laid out the cost, 200 for each filling x 3 teeth and 1500 for periodontal disease, 2100, God is good, almost exactly the amount I had got back on tax, again another huge relief! And off course cause God is better than we can ever imagine, the following week when I went back to have the first half of the procedure, the dentist says to the receptionist at the time of paying take 100 off, so total came to exact same amount I had gotten back on tax, go God! Not only had God come through for me with my declaration of cavities, he had come through for me in figuring out how I was going to cover the cost, something that had weighed so heavily on my mind for so long.

All these amazing blessing just resulted in my faith growing another notch, my understanding of how much God loves us grew greatly, my testimony bigger. I so very much wanted to make God proud of me, so I diligently read the Bible daily wanting to know Him more. I started praying morning and night, wanting to thank Him, know Him, and continued to ask for more wisdom. I was also starting to think it was time to find a church, fellowship was no longer enough, I needed to plant myself somewhere, but God already had plans I knew nothing about, I just need to keep looking for the path, and find it I did!

But first I'll tell the story of one more demon, that God helped me to beat. One that I had loved, and didn't see myself giving up. One that had had me by the balls for years, one that the Bible didn't specifically talk about as sin. But I was slowly creeping towards the idea that needed to be evicted, something that perhaps gave Satan a foothold in my life, a distraction, a financial burden that need to go, what was it you ask? Simple, cigarettes!

20 years had passed since I started smoking, I very much enjoyed it, the act of sitting alone, rolling a smoke, having those 5mins to myself had been an escape, a 5min break from life, where I got to be still, where conversations with strangers were started, an excuse to excuse yourself and leave a place. But I felt God was telling me it was time to stop, and for God I agreed, I would do anything.

I'd tried to evict the demon of addiction once before, but I don't think I had the full conviction then, you have to really want it. Want to be free, be desperate to be free, demons are happy to stay if they can find any excuse, and even happier to come back if you leave a door open, so I needed to be ready or it was never going to work.

As time had passed, I was stepping more and more into the authority God was showing me, through His word and faith. So, when I simply decided, the cigarette I held was the last one, the last I would ever smoke. I simply stated, "nicotine demon leave in the name of Jesus, addiction demon leave in the name of Jesus. I command you to the pit, in the name and the blood of Jesus. Praise Jesus, thank you Jesus" and truly meant it with all my heart, it was done. God is faithful. God is grace and mercy.

I didn't feel anything happen, there was no display, it just happened as simply as a few sentences spoken. I threw out the empty pack, threw out the ash tray, and stored the lighters in a draw, to be used next winter for the fire place. Then it was like I simply forgot; the habit was broken. I didn't have to fight the thoughts, or talk myself out if it. The voice in my head suggesting I needed a cigarette was gone, the action of rolling thousands of cigarettes, over the years put aside, forgotten, even the looking for a place or opportunity to excuse myself left.

The taste and smell I can't even recall, it was like I'd never smoked, it was like hearing about something that someone else did. The idea that I had been a cigarette smoker, for 20 years seemed untrue, like that person was someone else.

It's only been about 4 months, but seems like much much longer. I don't even think about smoking, if I was offered a cigarette I wouldn't even be tempted. It really blows my mind to be honest, not only how good God is, but how many powers he allows us to have here on earth, once we understand and step into them, but also how easily we fall for the devil's schemes, and just how many of them there are!

He did get me in one regard I suspect, but it was also needed, food! I'd dropped so much weight over previous 18 months, that once cigarettes were removed, I started eating. All stomach issues had resolved with stopping the antidepressants, so for first time in a long time I enjoyed eating, does food taste better when you stop smoking? I'm not sure to be honest, but food sure does taste better when you are not worried about getting sick, I will definitely say that much.

So, in last 4 months I've put on 15kgs, and am at a weight I should be, my clothes fit again, has it been enjoyable, absolutely. I literally ate what a wanted without a second thought, when does that ever happen. I've slowed down now, and am more conscious of not eating a block of chocolate daily. I'm also not riding 4 or 5 horses a day, so not burning it off either. My whole system has changed, so I need to figure out how much I can eat now, but that's fine, everything is a process, and if gluttony takes hold, I know I can evict it, I hope! Really food is the best lesson in self-control. It's too easy in today's society to eat, not like in days past, where producing a meal was a process and hard work in itself. Fasting is something that is very much biblical for a reason, it's good to show God at all times just how much he means to us, in ways beyond our spoken words, in ways we can crucify our own flesh, as Jesus did for us when he provided the beyond amazing gift of salvation. Amen, thankyou Jesus.

Lessons Learnt...

LESSON O

Persistence and patience

> "You need to persevere so that when you have done the will of God, you will receive what he has promised." Hebrew 10:36 NIV

> "Let's not get tired of doing good, because in time we'll have a harvest if we don't give up." Galatians 6:9

Much like learning the hard way, both Gods path and horses require a lot of patience and persistence.

Timing is so very important; we cannot rush God. God does things in His own timing; we often don't understand this timing as we are living it. We want things to hurry up, we want our prayers answered now. This is rarely the way, though when our prayers are finally answered it comes with understanding of why it had to be that way, the steps that had to be taken first, the things we needed to learn and understand first, the wisdom we needed to gain before we get our blessing, before we break free of the struggle, get our breakthrough.

Living it is not easy, we have to draw on all our patience, we have to hold ourselves in check, keep doing good, keep moving forward, keep being persistent, keep praying, keep reading the Bible, while not getting frustrated, not losing our patience. We must trust God, hold onto the fact

His timing is better than ours, we must continue to gain wisdom and keep learning, stay calm and never give up or turning away from God.

Horses taught me endless patience, their brains do not work like ours, we must wait to see if they have understood, wait til they trust us, wait till they relax, there is alot of waiting that requires patience. If they haven't understood, we must go over the same lesson, again and again, with quiet patience and persistence until they do understand, or we must change the way we are asking, never losing patience, never losing focus of the goal to help the horse. Every horse is different, they all have different histories, many have been taught the wrong thing, so they become fearful or reactive. We must remain calm, support them, never getting frustrated, never giving up, going as slowly as the horse needs, finding the right timing in communication with the horse, so the horse understands.

In ourselves we must keep learning, keep gathering the wisdom and understanding needed to help the horse. It's an endless learning journey, very much like our journey with God. It's not a straight line there are many ups and down, we must never lose faith, we must stay the course with patience and persistence, the rewards will come, a bountiful harvest.

LESSON P

Be teachable. Find wisdom

> "You have been given a teachable heart to perceive
> the secret, hidden mysteries of God's kingdom
> realm. But to those who don't have a listening heart,
> my words are mere stories." Luke 8 :10 TPT

God wants us to be teachable, there is so very much to learn, so much wisdom to be gained. People spend their whole lives studying the Bible and still have questions, are still being given new revelations by God as to another way of looking at something, another layer to learn, having a relationship with God is a lifelong learning journey, there is always more wisdom to be gained, it is a thrilling journey.

It is important to God that we are keen learners, because in this learning we become closer to Him, understand His word more clearly. God is OK with us being wrong but wanting to learn right, in order to do this, we have to be ok with being wrong, we won't always like what we are being told when we are wrong. But we must take it as a learning opportunity, we must use every opportunity to try to understand what God is trying to teach us. What new wisdom he is trying to impart on us, the hidden mysteries, it grows us spiritually, makes us more like Jesus. Wisdom allows more peace and joy into our lives, allows us better protection from the enemy, to stop us getting hurt, stop us getting attacked. God is happy to provide this wisdom, we only have to ask and learn, be teachable, have a listening heart.

Horses are another endless source of learning, if we are teachable and open to it. During my horse journey, I was mentored by a very experienced and brilliant horse trainer, John O'Leary. John is the old school type of teacher, he tells it like it is, if you are going to get upset with being told you are doing it wrong then you won't learn much, you have to be teachable and listen, absorb his endless knowledge. Take the opportunity to gain the wisdom that came through years of experience, 1000s of horses, there is so much opportunity to learn things that may take much longer if you are on your own.

I wanted to learn, and have no problem being told I'm wrong, corrected and learning from it. Being teachable like this, John was happy to mentor me. I never got defensive or tried to justify why I was wrong. I adsorbed the advice and learnt from it; this has continued on with my journey to God. God knows me better than anyone, he knows I've proved myself teachable, time and time again. God uses this gift he gave me, to advance my journey to know Him, which has been like nothing I've ever learnt before. Being teachable in lessons I didn't know I needed! Receiving answers to questions I've always had, the secret answers to the hidden mysteries, the things that make life make sense. Allow us to live in peace and joy with a sound mind.

Chapter 10

MERROO. A 20-YEAR WAIT.

"A huge cleared grass area. Acres among the trees. Bush land surrounding. Up higher on a mountain or big hill. One access road in. Accommodation for many. Young people staying there. Horses. The front entrance, two posts with another raised between."

This knowing had started in my 20s, I'd named it "the end of the world property" I had no idea where it was, how I would get there or what it meant. I pondered this vision over the years. I would have loved to live on 100 acres, have more room for the horses, but I always said I would never move the kids away from Mum again, after returning to Sydney after the fire. Though I never told her that, we were already living just under an hour away. Moving even another 30mins out, over the river, made the travel that bit too far to be doing regularly, it wasn't fair on the kids who loved seeing her so often, and they didn't have the same love of horses I did, there was no benefit to them living on a bigger property.

As I grew older, I also realised how hard it would be to care for such a large property alone. Especially as years of bush fire seasons passed and then we were hit with floods, the desire to be on a much larger property slowly faded. I was content to stay where we were, and like all knowings I had no idea how it would come to passed, but it never went away.

20 years passed, all other knowings had come true, new ones formed and came to pass, but this one just sat there. Did I doubt it would happen or think I had missed it, absolutely, but I could still see it in the back of my mind.

Time line wise it was now around June 2023. I had been to the Tim Hall revival and delivered been from death. I was very excited, my understanding of the power of God just grew and grew. Leigh from Hope Hub, whom had been at Tim Hall had decided to start a monthly Friday night worship. I had no idea what this meant, but when I was invited and offered a lift I jumped at the chance. I was always waiting for God to show me the way, show me what was next step. I wanted desperately to be obedient after how I had been blessed. I wanted more God in my life, to make Him proud.

Upon arrival there was maybe 10 people there, to my surprise Josie was also there. I sat down and introduced myself, Josie of course didn't remember me, she had delivered lots of people over the time in the tent revival, and befriended Leigh at the same time, no doubt an act of God! Everyone was chatting, and then there was an opening in the conversation where I testified. Excited to tell the outcome of the deliverance, my being healed, how God had blessed me, using Josie to deliver me from death. I blurted out me being a God newbie, and a how I'd been told I probably had lung cancer or lymphoma, only weeks before and now I'd got the results back. Benign. How shocked the specialist had been, it had worked God had in fact delivered me from death. I was on fire for God, I wanted to tell anyone and everyone one, other friends who didn't believe in God I'm sure thought I was mad, thought I was just lucky the doctors got it wrong, but I knew it was all God. Zero doubt.

The night though was a worship night, to my surprise as I didn't know what a worship night was, we spent the next few hours singing. I of course knew none of the songs! The amazingly talented Bec playing the piano. This was beginning of my worship understanding. I had grown up in catholic church, there was nothing like this there, only maybe a few old school hymns, but over time I understood this was a way to thank God, to glorify Him.

Afterwards was more fellowship. God does like to have a laugh with me, I can take a joke laugh at myself. I also tend to have a big mouth and am an over sharer, especially when it was something like what had happened with the deliverance. Among other believers I felt safe so off my mouth went, spilling out more of the story, maybe even that night God was using me, for confirmation to somebody else's question. As I'm learning happens a lot!

Good thing I was ignorant of who those other people were, they weren't just other friends of Leigh's, well they were her friends. But majority, especially the ones I had just testified too, were all pastors! As far as you could get from being God newbies like me, Eeeek! They all had or did have their own congregation, their own church. If I had known, there's no way I'd have blurted out my story like that. I'd have been to embarrassed, to self conscious, these feelings are not of God, so it would have meant Satan would have kept me silent, but God had other plans.

It also turned out one of the people there, an older gentleman, was the owner of the church next door to Leigh, Pastor David. Located on a huge acreage, called Merroo. Leigh had been telling me it had shut down over covid and was starting up again. My interest was piqued. I felt I owed it to

God to further my journey getting to know Him. Although I enjoyed the Tuesday fellowship group, I needed to take the next step. I needed to go to church. To plant myself in a church, but I was reluctant at best, the idea of a big group of people I didn't know caused concern, so that couldn't be God path, but God always has plans we know nothing about, plans better than we could even try to imagine. We just have to try to stay on the narrow path, not let Satan divert or distract us though our own emotions or other people, it's a far from easy thing to do!

Hearing Merroo was located up a big hill on acres, the knowing flashed in my mind, surely not I thought, as we drove past the entrance on the way home from Leigh's, I was disappointed to see there wasn't timber posts but bricks, not my vision after all. But I wasn't totally put off, I was willing to give it a go based on Leigh's excitement.

Leigh and I had met years beforehand, after Kris recommended me as a horse trainer, she had kept her own horses around the corner from my house for a period of time, when they had escaped, I'd gone to help. We didn't know each other well, but had many mutual friends, but of the Hope Hub ladies she had the most previous history and knowledge of deliverance, through personal experience and her family. Unlike some of the other ladies, who didn't share the same passion and revelation, and were inclined to being more suspicious and discouraging.

We were fast becoming better friends, she was someone I could ask dumb questions to and share experiences with, and if I was getting off track would nudge me back on the right track, without letting Satan throw feeling or offence into the mix. somethings especially related to ties with mental health, are not always well received. People don't like to hear their mental health is bad because of demonic oppression, and I totally understand that. Its pretty wild, people get offended and defensive, which is never the intention. But chatting with Leigh this wasn't the case. God had plans! We were both encouraging each other on the narrow path, and without connecting I may never have gone to the Tim Hall revival in the first place, definitely never too Merroo.

It would have been I guess a week or 2 later when I finally decided to go to a service at Merroo, my daughter wanted to come, if nothing else just to go for a drive. It was about 40mins drive from home. A very pretty journey through a rural area across the river, heading towards the blue mountains.

The night before we were due to go, I had a dream, my daughter and I were in the car driving along all these country roads, lost, up and back we went mightily confused about which way to go or where we were going, til finally we were confident we were finally on the right road, tall dark green trees lining either side of the road, end of dream.

I can't say I wasn't more than a little surprised, when the following day going to Merroo we were following the google maps lady and we got lost. We went way past where we were supposed to go, up some random country roads, then turning around we went in the brick entrance I had previously seen. Not knowing I was still in the wrong place, but there wasn't a human or car to be seen. We were a bit confused, so we further back tracked to another entrance we had driven past while listening to the google lady. This wasn't as well marked, and involved following a narrow road through the tall green trees. Ping my brain realised we had just lived my dream! Wow!

Upon following this private road, a single access road in, we came upon a timber entrance this time. But not the timber beam I'd seen you drove under, it then opened out to a large cleared acres, on the top of a hill, with a row of units lined up to provide accommodation for people if they wanted to come stay. Bushland surrounding. I wasn't expecting this!

There was centre 1 right ahead, followed by the function centre, where we needed to be that day. A lovely old timber hall, nothing much churchy about it, chairs had been set up. No pews nothing like my childhood church. I felt comfortable, welcome, not what I had been expecting.

It felt surreal being there, very much like I'd walked into the knowing, but my brain didn't want to believe that after 20 years I finally found it. It wasn't my property at all that I had seen. But if you had told me a few years earlier that "the end of the world property" from my knowing would have been a church I wouldn't have believed you. In fact, I would have very much resisted it, tried to stop that being the case even. Before I found God church was the last place I wanted to be, or could imagine myself being.

But let's face it, the knowings never turned out how I wanted. They always took me by surprise, and they always marked a big change or event in my life. Did this place, Merroo, begin a fulfilment of all these types of changes. Tick every box, yes absolutely it did, but still my brain resisted. Evil did not want me to believe a church has been my destiny. I think even Satan was shocked!

Then I saw it the confirmation I needed. the logo for the church. It looked like a gate, 2 poles with lines forming the roof, a child's drawing a symbol. That moment came like it did with all the knowings before, where time stood still, where you knew, it had come to pass. The knowing realised in reality, confirmation. it had in fact arrived no denying it now. I just hoped that cause God was finally involved, it would be a good change a marker on the narrow path.

Six months have now passed, from first going to writing this, such a short time in the grand scheme of things, but it feels like much longer. From that first visit I have rarely missed a Sunday. Though Satan sure does try and stop me, he hates me going, he uses the same tactic most weekends trying to make me feel sick or provide a human distraction. I've learnt now, once I get there, I always feel 100 % better, always! It's a learning experience in ignoring the enemy.

To my relief it's only a very small church, it's slowly growing, but the size has meant I've gotten to know everyone there. Made friends with people I wouldn't have otherwise, people where are only common interest is God, people of all ages and backgrounds, not just horse people for a change, not something I was expecting.

Although "the end of the world" property didn't turn out to be mine, it definitely feels like home, it's a very beautiful place, sitting on the top of a huge hill, surrounded by trees and native bushland. Across the road through the brick gate is the other section. Originally a PCYC youth centre built for young people for camps. It even includes the pony club grounds, currently unused. There's also a couple of elderly horses and closer to his house is stables left over from days the owner/pastor David's children were growing up there, they are now my age, long moved out.

More and more this place, Merroo, tick's boxes from that vision from 20 years ago. That I had wondered so long about, wondered how it would come about, the change it would represent. I now wonder what God plans are for the future, He sure does throw in a lot of curve balls!

It's so interesting how all the people now at Merroo seem to have their own story of how they got there. God talking and guiding them there. For many it's not their local church, they travel to get there, there's even others with dreams or visions. Yet others that have a history with the place, many visiting the Christian youth camps as children or teens, it's very fascinating, uplifting. Even Josie came and stayed, which I never would have predicted that day at Tim Hall revival, and she's far from home, travelling from the Northern Beaches a couple of hours away to hold service on Friday and Sundays. It's like Merroo chooses it people, well God really, they come see if they fit and get tested to see if they stay. The original pastor, from when I arrived even felt he needed to leave more recently, further opening the door for God to move. The Holy Spirit is thick in that place, everyone loves

God dearly, puts God first, those who don't, don't seem to stay long. God moves them on.

I'll often have a thought or a dream and the Sunday services often provides confirmation I wasn't even seeking, didn't know I needed. I'm continually amazed, I look forward to every week, know I will leave feeling joy, have questions answered, help me stay the course, walk the narrow path.

Even writing these words now. I had the words "God and horses" floating around in my head for a good 12 months. I really didn't understand. I kept trying to see how they fitted together, if it was a word a from God, or my own rolling thoughts. I thought at one stage the words could even be a business with a Christian friend. But I don't want to go back to horses without God being a part of it, without God getting the glory, when I try to take those paths that seem good ideas, I lose my peace and joy. I start to worry, if I have to try too hard to make it work, feel insecure. I've now learnt that's the wrong way. I've been diverted from the narrow path, so I don't know what the future holds work wise. God does though, I just need patience to wait.

Then God said to start writing my testimony, and it's only been 3 weeks to write this much. I was listening to Josie speak at Merroo, and her testimonies of God speaking to her when she was a younger and her child like faith to do the random things God might suggest. When it popped in my head that "God and horses " those words that had been rolling around in my head so long that I didn't understand were the name of a book, the name of my testimony, then when people looked up horses on Amazon this would slip through. Wait what? I thought, a book was not something I had considered. Though people often told me I should write a book of all the stories, of all the horses and crazy horse ladies I had met. I had previously written a few paragraphs of my finding God testimony but it felt disjointed and I had struggled. A few days after this service after having that idea put in my head, I picked up my phone and started to write, these words have just poured out, no doubt, no worry I knew it was from God. With all credit to the Holy Spirit helping, it wasn't like when I tried to write before. I'm shocked at how easily this has come together. There had been so many twisted and turns in my life over the last couple of years, memories return as I write. How things had seemed so dark just before they are just about to get better. On days I don't write Satan has a go, he will try and throw in doubts, stop me from continuing, but that's to be expected now. He certainly doesn't want any testimony out there, it's a weapon against him, but days I do write I live in the peace and joy. It drives me forward to continue; it feels like the right path. I have hope that my words will be the thing someone else needs to find God. To have their own peace and joy, their own relationship with Him, that gets them saved, even the Bible says that much, so onward I write, trusting God has a plan for my words, even if they are just for one person.

Merroo has been the blessing I was looking for to further my own relationship with God, the worship music and singing I now enjoy and doesn't come as a shock. I'm not just waiting til it's over, I feel it. I also enjoy listening to the words different people speak, the messages they bring, the Bible has endless layers and people's testimonies add to it, bring more understanding, bring life to the words. I also really enjoy the fellowship after the service, making friends and talking about God. I'm usually there half of the day. Slowly my kids are joining me, going for me is a priority now, a must, not something I do on a Sunday morning before the day starts, like I hear other people speak about church as, which is a shame they are missing so much God. They are missing out on getting filled up with the Holy Spirit that wonderful feeling, better than any drug. God is my number one priority, not kids sport or horses. It's crazy how much I have changed; I could never have imagined myself this way even 12 months ago. Old Nicole would be laughing at new Nicole wondering if she has lost her mind, new Nicole just feels sorry for old Nicole, as she's doesn't know what she doesn't know, and certainly doesn't know what she is missing out on, the one thing she always wanted, peace.

Leigh also began a weekly women's group of Merroo ladies, which is very different from the fellowship of the other ladies of Hope Hub. Hope Hub involved chat and catch up, support for each other. God is at the end, if at all, it's about us not him, trying not to scare people away from God by having too much God. It was very much a key God used for me to gain wisdom, and He will no doubt use for others, a huge blessing, it is wonderful thing they are doing, creating a space for God to open a door into lives without him. For women to get saved.

The Merroo ladies is completely different, it's totally about worship to God and prayer for each other, with coffee and catch up after, time permitted. Warrior prayer women I'm often amazed, a group of women who met at Merroo, all having given their lives to God already, somewhere I can further get to know God. Deepen my relationship with Him yet again, I'm learning so much from them, while God is blessing us all with signs and wonders of deliverance and healings, especially when new women come in.

All the ladies I've met in both groups have been a huge blessing in my walk with God. I've needed each and every one, God has been very good to me.

It's all part of my narrow path journey, I needed one to group to reach the other, without the Hope Hub I would never have gone to church in the first place. I would have resisted fellowship, and that's not the way it's supposed to be. We are not supposed to walk alone, without them I would never have found Merroo, and in turn met another group of strong

Godly women from whom I can continue to learn, whom are much further along their walk with God than I am. Mature Christians, it's all been part of Gods plan. With everybody I have met, my wisdom has continued to grow. Just like I prayed for, and I'm most definitely learning how to pray finally, morning and night without fail, I'm learning about the secret place. I have a genuine fear of God, a genuine thanks, I want to make God proud, to honour Him. I've also committed to reading the Bible daily. I've read it through, now am going back trying to gain greater understanding, strengthen my spirit man, gain more needed wisdom, learn the word, sharpen my sword.

I called Merroo the "end of the world" property for 20 years, before I ever set foot there, before the world had changed to what it is now, before covid, before floods, before I even knew Bible prophecy was a thing. Now the world has started to feel like its heading more and more in that direction every day, the end of the world and Jesus' return feels very close. What comes next is not my worry, that is what God is for, my Father looking out for me, the relief in understanding just that is immense. I'm like a child again, living under my parents' roof, or dwelling as the Bible says, with no concern of tomorrow, all my faith in God.

I still wait for the next knowing to come to pass when I least expect it. "Myself standing behind another women while she looks out over people standing on a grass area, them all looking towards her listening to her words" but I also know that whatever I guess will be wrong, except for the fact another big change will come, so for now I say thankyou God, please keep showing me the way, the difference these days is I wait on God with anticipation, with hope for the future.

Lessons Learnt...

LESSON Q

Put others first

> "Do nothing out of selfish ambition or vain conceit, but in humility consider others better than yourselves." Philippians 2:3 NIV

Put your horse first, before you look after yourself, look after your animals, they need you to help them, they rely on you for everything, for survival. They are your responsibility, their needs come before your own, rain hail or shine.

The Lord teaches to put other people before yourself, no questions asked. We need to help others, when and where we can, helping others may take a toll on ourselves, but sacrifice is a must on our journey with God. We must not look for what we can get out of a situation before we step in, we need to use our good hearts towards everyone, we don't know when our stepping into help someone will be their key to survival.

LESSON R

Stay humble

> "Humble yourselves before the Lord, and he will lift you up." James 4:10 NIV

Working with horses has been a huge privilege, it's hard work and not easy, but it has always been important to stay humble, to never feel entitled, to be willing to learn more as the trials and challenges will never end. To ask for help from those with greater wisdom than you, because there will always be another horse that comes along to show you how much you don't know. No doubt sent by God!

It's important to always be excited by new challenges horses bring, not upset by them, it is a way to achieve more wisdom, become a better trainer, to be the best you can be. As soon as ego and pride kick in, and we don't want to find another way, or ask for help we are already going backwards, we are blocking our own path to learning more.

Horses have always kept me humble, I always wanted to be the most effective trainer I could be.

This horse lesson has been a great blessing in my journey with God, it feels like a huge privilege to be developing a relationship with Him, to be sent the knowings and dreams, to hear His voice, I never take it for granted.

I've learnt I will need help, to reach out to others with questions, no matter how silly they may sound, to not be prideful, to ask those with the wisdom I need, comfortable to be corrected, never thinking I'm special or could that I do any of this without God.

The horses taught me that the trials and challenges won't ever stop, so enjoy them. With God new trials mean greater blessings are coming. I must stay humble, take nothing for granted, allow God to transform me through these trials. Do not resent how hard things may be, only God can allow me to become more effective in the kingdom, to become a better warrior against evil, an inspiration for others, to themselves want to become closer to God, when they see the amazing work God is doing in me, always giving all glory to God, for I am nothing without Him.

Chapter 11

DREAMER OF DREAMS.

I guess I've always been a dreamer, not a dreamer like of the future or of good things coming, but a dreamer as in during sleep at night.

I was told many times that when I was a child, I never slept a night through til I was 8. I have no doubt that was because of nightmares. I'm not sure if the abuse from the neighbour was a trigger, as I don't know how old I was when this started, but it no doubt played a big part.

In my understanding now of dreams and demons. We come under an attack in the spiritual, before it manifests in the physical. So, a bad dream may be a warning of depression or anxiety for example. Demons are allowed to come in and attack based on spiritual legal rights, doors that are open, or footholds given, which happen in the physical realm. Abuse is one of the ways demons get access to our minds, through fear and shame. It's like a merry go round, something happens in the physical for example, a sin like lieing or unmarried sex, this opens the door in the spiritual. Gives demons legal right to attack, this then manifests in the physical in say an anxiety attack, which makes us miserable. Then Satan has us right where he wants us. God would never have us feel this way but sin allows it. It's why it's so important to not sin, we just make our own lives harder, this is how free choice works. God tries to show us the way to live lives of peace and joy, but we choose to sin, and end up feeling how Satan wants us to feel, closer to hell.

Doors can also be left open through others sin towards us, like abuse, as it triggers emotions which are not from God, pain and fear are two of these open doors. They come in and get a grip, a foothold in our minds. Children especially are very vulnerable, for me the abuse no doubt allowed this door to be opened and foothold gained, that would last the next 40 years, before I finally learnt how to keep it shut! How to evict those demons of the past with deliverance, a gift from Jesus sacrifice.

Word and generational curses also play a part, allow evil access, so my being told constantly growing up what a difficult child I was, what a burden I was, waking up my mother through the night for so long, how my anxiety made my parents angry at me for being out of control. Just strengthened the hold evil had on my mind, both through nightmares and my mental health.

There are a few nightmares in particular I vividly remember I had as a child, even now they are as clear as day.

The first was being chased, I was always being chased, it was always dark in the dream. I would be running along the street, usually my parent's street, and trying to fly away. I'd run a few steps and try and take off, in the dream I knew I could fly, sometimes I did fly, other times I'd be frustrated why I could not. I was always scared, whatever was chasing me never got me, but sometimes it seemed to continue for a long long time. In the dreams where I could fly, I would still be chased, whatever was after me could also fly. These chases felt like they went on for ages, I was terrified and would look over my shoulder, trying to see if I had escaped yet, but never seeing what was chasing me. These were awful nightmares of which I had hundreds, all through my life, as a child I must have woken screaming, waking my mother.

The second type of dream, and I had one of these recently again which was concerning, was that there is a magnetic force pulling me towards the road, it starts suddenly. I would be walking down the street then it would start. I can't escape it. I hold onto things trying to stop the force moving me, from dragging me out in front of traffic, no one else in the dream is ever under the same force. No one seems to notice that I am in trouble, no one ever helps me, this type of dream like flying dream has occurred many different times in many different ways, there is usually cars or buses coming towards me that I am trying to avoid getting hit by.

But there is one variation that as a child I had over and over again. Dream: myself, my mother and brother are walking along the street near her house. Simple one-story houses line the street, we head towards the shop up the street, the force comes. I am being pulled towards the road, cars are driving down the street, my leg gets hit by a car, removing my foot, there is no blood, simply I no longer have a foot. The force stops, I get back off the road, my brother and mother have continued walking along the street, not noticing what has happened. My mother calls to me, annoyance in her voice, telling me to hurry up. I stumble after them trying to walk, but it is very difficult as I am missing a foot. End dream.

The third type of dream I used to have over and over again was needing to go to the toilet. I would be in different places, from the shopping centre to fun parks, and desperately need the toilet. I would ask people for directions, but no matter how far I ran and how desperately I looked I could never find a toilet. Interestingly I've now learnt using a toilet in a dream represents deliverance.

The final dream from childhood I remember vividly having multiple times was always the same. Its always disturbed me. It's night time again I'm walking down the street, returning home to my parents. It's dark, very dark, the only light coming from the street lights, as I pass the house next door their garage door is open, the light is on, and there stands the neighbours son, in real life he's much older than me, in the dream he is hammering, hitting something metal something heavy. I can hear the noise, the high-pitched clanging ringing out as he hammers, a slow steady sequence, over and over, bang, bang, bang, he looks up and sees me coming, stares at me, fear hits me. I am terrified to pass his house, to get to my own and safety. End dream.

Even now thinking back, this dream disturbs me. I don't think I was ever abused by this man; the abusive neighbour was female and lived across the road not next door, or I have no memory of the abuse, but it sure induced fear. One of Satan's favourite emotions.

All these dreams in fact induce emotions that are not from God. Mainly fear. They are all attacks in the spiritual realm, all manifesting emotions that would carry across into the physical world, and torment me for years, until I found God, and the gift of deliverance, which allowed me to renounce these past traumas, to finally learn how to close those doors, to stop those awful nightmares which had tormented me for so many years. But once I had deliverance the dreams didn't stop in fact the dreams started to ramp up, become increasingly frequent, taking over my life even!

The Bible says in the last days old men will dream dreams, apparently, I'm one of those old men! Maybe Satan always knew this, maybe that's why he came for me so young, to keep me far away from ever finding God, from walking the narrow path, to torment me as much as possible before I learnt how to fight back.

It's been about 6 months now, not long after Mum died, about April 2023, maybe more since the dreams escalated. Before then, not getting deep sleep, drinking, being unwell, perhaps the antidepressants even, but for a long time, years even. I barely remembered my dreams, considering they were mostly nightmares I was happy for that to be the case. I didn't think much of it, I was so unwell, the days often felt like a living nightmare I had to survive, sleep was an escape, if that that been a constant nightmare as well, then maybe my brain would have completely broken.

It started with me waking up multiple times through the night. Knowing I'd had a dream, but not really remembering it, then not being able to get back to sleep. I would toss and turn for what felt like hours, which anyone who's experienced this will tell you is a waking nightmare, extremely frustrating, being so very tired but not being able to sleep, you never feel rested.

Then I noticed it, the time. I was always waking at the same time, midnight and then 3am. So, I googled it, as you do, to my surprise I discovered this was witching hour. The time where anyone working for the other side, anyone even in their ignorance of what witchcraft was, was worshipping Satan. Crikey I thought, these people are much more committed than many Christians. Christians can barely get to church on a Sunday, these people were up all night worshipping their evil idols.

I hadn't found Merroo yet, nor had I started really praying, but God was about to show me it was time to step up. So, I looked up how to come against these spiritual attacks which seemed to be coming for me. I wanted my sleep back, so I needed to learn how to pray against it. I knew God was endlessly more powerful than evil.

I started by copying the prayers I found, onto the computer note pad, which meant I could read them in the dark. Every time I got woken in the night, especially during the hours of 12 and 3am. I started to pray, these massively long prayers. I would often pray for over an hour, reading aloud the words, to cancelled out and send fire and angels to defeat the evil being aimed at me. After which I'd be able to fall back asleep, it was obviously working so I kept it up. Every night, every time I would be woken, I would pray, seeking God's help.

Then over the next few weeks, something else changed. I started to be able to remember dreams, just once or twice a week at first, then more and more. I was still getting woken through the night, I'd pray and wonder about the dream, but come morning much to my frustration, I could no longer remember the dream.

Easy fix I thought, I'll write them down. I kept a physical note pad and pen next to my bed. As soon as I would wake through the night, I'd write it down. Then almost straight away Id fall back to sleep. I probably should have kept praying, but I like to learn the hard way. Satan will absolutely use sleep against you! Easiest way to feel this is try reading the Bible, instantly you feel dopey and want a nap. Satan does not want you reading Gods word, the spirit of tiredness will come against you.

Now I had the dreams written down, usually one or two every night or two, other nights Id started sleeping through. I found all this very exciting and upon waking in the morning I would try and figure out what they meant. I had enough sense to know I needed Bible interpretations not new age ones. I'd also look up key things in the dream in the actual Bible, and search for Christian dream interpretation.

An example being a dream about yogurt, lots of tubs lined up. in Bible it talks about milk being fed to baby Christians as they weren't ready for full meal, at the time I was seeing myself less and less as a baby Christian. I'd learnt so much, about deliverance and healing, I'd read the whole Bible almost! As is always the way, I didn't know what I didn't know. I was very much a baby still. I wondered if I was still only getting milk, what was the full meal. I asked God for more wisdom. I was really enjoying what felt like open line of communication with God, every morning the first thing I wanted to do, looked forward to doing was figuring out these dream meanings, find the message from God.

Then things started getting out of control, as much as I loved hearing from God. Satan hated it, we humans don't really understand how much Satan hates us, we under estimate that hate.

The dreams are an opening into the spiritual, what happens in the spiritual then happens in the physical, many dreams are a gift from God, a cheat sheet even. A window into the trouble Satan is trying to cause, and because God gifts us the power to tread on evil, on serpents and scorpions. We then can defend ourselves, we can defeat him before he can send demons to torment us, before he can send demons that will block and delay the blessings God has for us, by triggering us, making us short tempered, angry, having unforgiveness or being offended. Any emotion not of God, all of which delays God blessing, diverts us from the narrow path.

So my one or two dreams, started to ramp up, now I was having 5 or 6 or 7, some nights 9 different dreams in one night. I knew it was this many, because I was still waking up, writing them down then going back to sleep. I would wake in the morning, and count them, shocked. It was starting to take hours to try and figure out meanings, and more and more the meanings weren't good, they were all representing attacks from evil, all showing Satan was trying to stop me having a breakthrough, this went on for months.

I was exhausted, my sleep was so broken up, the dreams which had felt like such a blessing now began to feel like a burden. I wanted them to stop. I was really struggling. I didn't stop writing them down, I still wanted to know when God was talking. I prayed for more wisdom.

The wisdom came when I started looking harder, I started stumbling across videos that explained what was happening, explained I was at war. Though no doubt this was act of God. The videos explained I had a window into the spiritual world, explained what dreams were hidden attacks, explained I needed to fight back, and to fight back I needed to be stronger in spirit. I needed to lean into God harder, surrender more, read the Bible more, and most importantly pray more, to learn how to pray into the word into Gods promises, there was alot of work still to be done, but I was 100% committed.

Slowly my perspective changed back, where I had been struggling and dreading the dreams, I learnt to accept them, I learnt I was being given a huge blessing from God. A warning system that evil was coming, that I was going to get attacked, to prepare for battle. I learnt that gifts from God come at the price of pissing off the enemy. I learnt that Satan did not want me to have these blessings and would come charging at me at every turn, trying to block the break through that would eventually come. I learnt I had to push on, keep going, keep learning, keep fighting. No matter how long it took, the Holy Spirit, God and Jesus had my back. The less Satan wanted me to have it, the more it was worth fighting for! Like the horses had taught me, keep going, don't let our minds be our own worst enemy, that was not of God.

God wants to give us every blessing due, don't turn away, make the choice, choose God, fight! I will win this war, learn how-to put-on Gods armour, is any of this easy? Heck no. Is it worth it? A million percent yes, everything from God is always more than worth it.

So how exactly was Satan coming for me, what were these dream attacks, how was I being tricked and attacked in the spiritual. The dreams I experienced as a child, of being chased, and the magnetic force towards the road were the most obvious types of attacks. They stir up feelings from

Satan, negative feelings, feelings like fear, anxiety, dread, and as my wisdom grew were easy to identify. It was the other dreams that I needed more wisdom to figure out, that I needed to pray against them.

Eating in dreams, something I never would have considered, I mean whom doesn't want to eat and enjoy food without the calories as you can in dreams, but it turned out these eating dreams have been one of the main types of dreams I seemed to be getting tricked in. A way in which evil uses to get me to accept something and then take it into my body, a covenant, they can cause mental and physical health issues, in the physical realm, and they did!

These dreams have come in soooo many different forms, from being in a restaurant and served food and eating it, to being at someone's house for dinner, to buying food in a shop, to it being a hot day and being offered an ice block. Once I found out these dreams were in fact spiritual attacks, then it was frustrating when they happened, and in the dream, I kept eating the food.

As soon as I realised, I would wake up and straight away, say a prayer to cancel the dream, to evict the food from my body to rebuke the attack. But I often found I would feel sick and tired in the following days, that if I had accepted something into my body in the dream that would affect me negatively in the physical.

Over time the eating dreams become less and less, but they still come back, even tricker, offering me something I would really love to eat in the physical, like an amazing chocolate cake or pastry! I'd then wake up saying dang it got me, sometimes though I'd not eat the food, which was progress, but mainly with a lot of prayer these dreams have decreased. Spiritually I'm getting stronger. I pray and read the Bible nightly getting ready for battle! Glad when I wake up having not eaten the food offered in my dream.

Another type of spiritual attack dream that came were sex dreams. Though I'm relieved to say these only came for a short period of time, and apparently my spirit man in this regard was already strong, as I always rejected every advance for sex in dreams. Though have on occasion been caught out with a kiss. I remember once particular night of dreams, over and over there were extremely good-looking men trying to hit on me, whom I kept rejecting. The final man in the dreams got very frustrated! Telling me he had wanted me all night and that I would have loved it. I woke up quite amused. Nicole 1, demons 0. Finally something I had won, beaten evil at it's own game!

I had also read about attacks that came in dreams where needles were involved. I hadn't had one of these, until I started telling people about my dreams, then all of a sudden, I was dreaming about getting recommendations to get Botox needles all inside my mouth to stop wrinkles they told me, quite fascinating really. Botox paralyses, so in the dream they were definitely trying to shut me up in the physical realm. Paralysis of my mouth, evil didn't want me telling others of my dreams, especially when they were a warning for them.

Dream interpretation is a gift unto itself, understanding the dreams is still mostly complicated and confusing. Most of my learning besides research has come from hindsight, something will happen in the physical and I'll look back through my dream records (there's now over 500 dreams recorded) and find a dream from a couple of weeks or month beforehand that had been an attack or a warning, either from God or Satan. I pray for wisdom to better understand as they happen rather than hindsight! Hindsight hurts!

Then there were dreams that represented my house, but not my actual house from real life. I had all different types of buildings in these dreams, from my understanding your home in dreams can often represent one's self. These buildings changed over different dreams, sometimes I would see damage to them like floods or termites which again would represent I was in trouble. I needed a stronger foundation in God, but the changing buildings also seemed to represent how much I was also changing as time passed, with damage to buildings showing how the evil attacks were taking their toll, again I knew I just needed to be stronger in spirit, a foundation built in stone.

The most amazing type of dream, God dreams, also came early on, during the time I was waiting on the lung cancer results. In the dream I was in a doctor's offices, paperwork was stacked to the ceiling, people from the past were there in the waiting room as well, girls I had gone to high school with. I was waiting for my turn, finally I was called. I followed the doctor down different winding corridors, he kept looking back making sure I was following, a look of love on his face which I found very concerning, didn't understand, why was a doctor looking at me like that. Finally, we existed the building into a court yard, a garden, the doctor turned smiling and gave me a big bear hug, this dream really confused me. End dream.

Then the next day I had a conversation with a friend, she shared a story about reading an article on a little girl having a dream and then drawing a picture of Jesus, upon opening the article, that was him! That was the doctor in my dream. Jesus! Wow, wow, wow. God sure does give confirmations in some amazing ways.

Jesus had shown up to lead me out of the chaos of the doctor office, to a quiet place, to comfort me, and the look of love from Jesus explained everything. Jesus loved me. Any concern I had since being delivered from death, to when I got those lung cancer results slipped away. I knew I would be fine, Jesus had me, He was there for me, even when I didn't recognise it was Him, so, so amazing.

Falling dreams also happened a few times. I would wake up before I hit the ground. But one dream stands out, and that was Jesus reaching out a hand to catch me. This time I knew it was Jesus. I had fallen from a great height, off the side of a road, and just as I was getting closer to the ground, He reached out His hand. I grabbed His hand, and he allowed me to land on my feet on the ground, I threw myself at His feet, praising Him thanking Him. This dream had to be from God. I was thrilled. God was telling me no matter if I fell Jesus would catch me. Jesus had already saved me. Jesus dreams are the best! I wake up feeling so alive.

Both these Jesus dreams are still so clear in my mind, like they happened yesterday not months ago, such an amazing message such a blessing.

Then there were the dreams when angels showed up, I didn't know this at first, as angels show up in my dreams as police! In the physical, these dreams have meant something bad happening in reality, but all the chaos and negative is needed, and in the end turns out to have caused a positive change. Something hidden is revealed, but now police dreams make me extremely cautious and concerned of just how crazy the physical reality will get. Even when I know it will turn out for the best, there's nothing fun about it.

Another type of dream that seems to occur alot is driving, or riding a bike somewhere. These seem to represent my journey in life, how I am progressing. Dreams where my car is stolen. Where the road is rough or I am lost, again show me things will get that way in the physical. To pray against it, and keep going towards God, don't let Satan divert me, don't let Satan keep me from the narrow path as he's going to try, constantly! Potholes and overgrown road doesn't mean I'm going in the wrong direction, just because the going is getting rough, don't be discouraged, push on, towards God.

There's also been driving and bike dreams, where I know exactly where I'm going. Where I may even go to church, or prayer meeting, where I'm taking my kids or friends with me. These dreams let me know I'm going the right way, doing the right thing, are uplifting, and confirmation to keep moving forward, that I'm on the right path, phew! Thank God.

Finally, there's the craziest dreams of all. I still don't always recognise them when they happen, again it's often hindsight, but I'm learning these dreams seem to have people in my life who are currently in my life, my real life in the physical.

These dreams are the prophetic dreams... dreams that come true in real life. These dreams still blow my mind, getting that sneak peek into the future, they involve both good and bad outcomes. A different type of knowing, as they happen much quicker, knowings take years to come to pass, the dreams only weeks or months, more recently days. As these dreams involve people I know. I'm always wondering if I am supposed to tell them the dream. If the dream is the answer to a question, they have asked God, as time passes, I speak these dreams more and more.

Here's a few dreams and how they came to pass, others are not for sharing, as I have ended up getting a view into people's private lives, even just telling people I had a dream about them at first seemed so odd so uncomfortable. But things seemed to have slowly changed, I tend to be much more open now, less concerned about people's reaction, and not just that, more and more people are coming to tell me their own dreams, which is awesome, especially as the Bible says in end times old men will dream dreams, all us women are old men too!

The thing that makes the dreams hardest to interpret, they are not usually literal, though occasionally that does happen, more often than not they are signs of events that come to pass, keys. You may see someone you know in the dream, they look different, maybe an extreme change of appearance, like pink hair, or punk clothes. Which translates in real life, as them presenting an attitude or behaviour that you don't recognise that you are shocked at, as shocked as you were seeing them with pink hair.

Another example being going to someone's house, out the back is a river of dark murky water. The kids are swimming, you feel it's dangerous, this translates in real life to the same person having a very dark times in their family, their marriage or their health. Something that they are keeping hidden out the back, or is hidden from them, something that is, or will, very much effect or is affecting their children, a dark place in their life.

So much in dreams are warnings of dark times ahead. One of the first prophetic dreams that I had, was when all the dreams started to escalate. It stuck in my memory and I was mighty shocked when it came true.

Dream: I was in a large dining hall type establishment, with many tables. I was looking for somewhere to sit, all of the tables were full, there was one table left that had space, only 2 ladies were sitting there. I approached them asking them if could join them, no they said I wasn't welcome. I was taken aback, but happily went to look for somewhere else to sit. End dream.

It was about 2 weeks later I was with a group of friends in a crowded cafe, there was some discussion and debate in regards to mental health, the two sides having very different opinions, this led to a split in the group. One of the ladies was so taken aback and decided she would not return to the group, she would no longer be joining us, but wasn't upset about the situation taking it all in her stride.

As the situation unfolded the dream flashed in my mind, I blurted it out. I dreamt this. I was taken aback not sure what it all this meant, could I have prevented it. Why was God showing me, I still don't know! But it did lead to me voicing my dreams to people much more, I want to be obedient to God, but do get confused what that involves sometimes. I don't want to get it wrong! I don't want to upset anyone if I do, it can be very surreal.

Another dream I had, I wasn't sure whether it was prophetic for a long time. So, I didn't speak it, but unlike a lot of dreams it stuck in my head. I had no trouble remembering.

Dream: I am with my son, he is younger maybe 7 or 8, he is walking I am on a bike, we are travelling down a gravel road. To our left are flats 4 or 5, like a motel, all joined together one after the other. There is no grass only gravel and sand out the front, there are a group of 5 cars parked, one is a white 4x4, to our right is trees, dense bush lining the road. It feels like we are up high, as we travel down the road, the flats and cars become like an old cartoon, where the back ground is repeated as the characters travel along, usually in a chase scene, over and over again the same background image, in the dream the same 4 or 5 flats the same cars parked, this repeats about 10 times as we travel down the gravel road, finally we come to the end, across the drive at a right angle to the flats is another building, with a porch and glass door. We climb the stairs and open the door, there is a woman standing there, talking to a group of people adults and children who are seated, we interrupt, she looks at us shocked at the interruption, we apologise, close the glass door. End dream.

The truth of this dream took quite a while to put together, the dream occurred at the time I had just started attending Merroo. It was a week two later the penny dropped, as you drive into Merroo there's a row of flats on the left, trees to the right, we are up high, at the end on the row a building at a right angle to the road, where we have been meeting for service, you enter through sliding glass doors. Ping my brain drew the link. Interestingly, when I first started going, the service was run by a male pastor whom has now left (on a word from God), and as time has passed women have taken over. The service is now mainly headed by women for the first time ever, a woman talking to a group of adults and children seated.

Was the dream prophetic, it sure feels like it. With the repeating buildings representing the same way things were run over the years again and again, with a male pastor as head, until women stepped in to take over more recently, this has continued with more and more women coming in taking responsibilities, it feels very God led.

Another Merroo dream, came a couple of months later.

Dream: I was driving on a highway, 3 lanes each way, there were very few other cars, the road went up and down, up and down then up a very big hill. Travel was easy, smooth but I went a long way, at the top was a very big sign saying FRESHWATER, and lots and lots people happily congregating there, almost like a village, end dream.

At the Merroo service the following week, I received an important phone call and had to leave early, missing the finally word from pastor David, the elderly owner of Merroo. It was later in the week I was sharing my dream with Leigh, about travelling towards freshwater, that she stopped me and said you mean like pastor David was talking about during service. Wait what I said. It turns out I'd missed the confirmation of the dream; Pastor David had been talking about Merroo moving from murky water of the past to freshwater. Amazing go God! Merroo also means "a place of a spring of water welling up ", which is freshwater, something I had completely forgotten. I was very humbled by God blessing me with these dreams, especially positive ones like this.

Note added here: After completion of my book, it's the middle December, conversation with Josie, telling her about this dream. Her turn to wait what! The previous day she had been on the Merroo office computer, an old document titled Freshwater was on the computer, how many years that had been on the computer or for what reason we don't know, but with God there is so coincidence. It was another confirmation of where all of us at Merroo are headed, into Freshwater. Amen, thank you Jesus.

Merroo and its people seem to be a common thread for positive prophetic dreams. Christine is a fellow prayer warrior of Merroo. Seven months earlier, she had had a mini cyclone come through her property, taking out the power lines. So had been living for 7 months with no power, battling the insurance company who were refusing her claim, causing her endless stress, she was practically camping in her own home.

Dream: the prayer group was having a meeting at her house, there was workmen everywhere, fixing the property. End dream. About 3 or 4 weeks passed, she turned up to prayer meeting very emotional, finally testifying that all our prayers for her had been answered. All of a sudden, the insurance company had changed their mind approved the claim. The workmen would be coming to fix her power! Praise God, another prophetic dream fulfilled, so humbling. God is so faithful, so kind, so good.

Then there are the dreams you really don't understand until later.

Dream: standing in the middle of a city with a group of people, surrounded by abandoned apartment buildings, tall and grey, feels like danger, we need to hide and escape, we enter one of the buildings. I see its foundation is cracked, I hit it, it fails, the building begins to collapse. We run, as we are running to safety, I look at my wrist at a watch, it is running in reverse, time is going backwards. End dream.

This dream occurred at the end of September 2023. 2 weeks later war broke out between Israel and Gaza. I can only guess safety for the people lies in the past, as has happened in the past the people need to turn back to God for safety. Cry out for God their saviour, to find Jesus. I pray for all their souls, that they turn to the Lord, accept Jesus as their salvation finally.

It's now the end of October, and this dream is most recent as I write, last night in fact. I dreamt I'd had a colonic, and the lady performing it was praying over me, a good thing in a dream, as toilet use represented problems and challenges leaving body, but as I mentioned the dream the next morning at the women's prayer meeting, one of the ladies piped up, saying that's exactly where she was going that very day, as soon as we finished. For a colonic! hoping it would help with stomach issues she was experiencing. We were both a bit shocked. I'm not exactly sure what this represented, perhaps that the colonic would help her stomach issues if we prayed like in the dream. Maybe her stomach issues were a spiritual attack, or more likely God is telling me things are speeding up, dreams which took months or weeks to come to pass, could now occur in next 24 hours, time to take notice, be on alert.

I've now filled 3 note books with dreams, well over 500, some are quickly forgotten other stick in my mind. It's hard to keep track, unlike the knowings which took years to come to pass, the dreams are coming to pass much quicker, and there's so many more of them, unlike before when I wished they would stop, now if I wake up without having written a dream, I worry I've missed something. Forgotten an important message, had it blocked by Satan. Every morning when I wake, I pray against any bad seed Satan is trying to plant in my life, cancel anything bad, and have become more confident that if I need to remember a dream, God will ensure I don't forget.

I'm still no less amazed when my dreams do come to pass, no less shocked. It feels like a gift, but then I wonder why me, why has God chosen me for this gift? But I guess being an over sharer helps! I wonder if all those years of the knowings, were preparing me for this, or if it's always been happening, and I just didn't remember, or forgot my dreams? Did Satan know something, and so made my dreams nightmares, chased me from them? Made them something horrid and fearful? So, I didn't realise the blessing, so I didn't find God sooner? Or was it his chance to attack, before I found the protection only God can provide. Jesus.

Those questions I'll never have the answer to. The Bible says don't look backwards, don't live in the past, don't be Lots wife and turn to salt. I understand this more and more as time passes, when we are not facing Jesus, when we are looking at the past, it triggers emotions, usually negative, sometimes even regret to leave that path, the past. It allows Satan a foothold, a distraction, a diversion, we then wander off Gods path, away from the peace and joy most people so desperately are looking for. They call it happy; they want to be happy, but they are looking for the wrong thing. I would never like to go back down that path again, away from God, to again fall off the narrow path of God's. To fall back into sin, it's so easy to do, think we are supposed to look for happiness. Pride especially, is ready to grab our hand, lead us off in the wrong direction, we are told to be proud of ourselves, not realising it steals our lives, we lose our peace and joy, our sound mind, God's promise.

So, I share my dreams with people now, as best I can. I hope it gives people hope, prepares them for the coming attack, turns them more to God, opens up their own minds for their own dreams, so that they too write them down, ponder them, don't just wake up and forget, go about their days. I pray this helps them grow closer to God, maintain their own peace and joy, the gift Jesus died for, saving us from ourselves. Praise God.

Lessons Learnt...

LESSON S

Don't look backwards

> "Forget the former things; do not dwell in the past.
> See I am doing a new thing!" Isaiah 43:18-19 NIV

As part of our healing journey with God as part of our learning and breaking free of demons of evil, of finding a new way a new path, we do look backwards, we repent and renounce all the sin of the past, we go over our lives looking where we went wrong, so we don't repeat them in the future.

But as the Bible says we must not live in the past; we must not look backwards with regret. Lots wife looked back and turned to salt. It only causes heart break to look back with regret or longing. Especially when we pine for the way things were. We must look forward towards God, we must not allow Satan to get a hold of us, and to drag us backwards, to fill our minds with the past. It is not of God it steals our peace and joy. The past is something we cannot change, once we are reborn the past has no relevance any more, we are free of the past and must live that way.

It can be much the same with horses, it is easy to look backwards, especially as years pass, and think I wish I had done this or that differently. Especially as you learn more and have hindsight, but we must not do this, we cannot change things, there is no point having regrets, we must move on and help the horse we have now, with the knowledge gained from the past, not beat ourselves up, wishing we had that chance again to do things differently. Like with our God journey, it only steals the joy of where we are now, of how far we have come.

LESSON T
Persecution

> "Blessed are those who are persecuted for righteousness sake, for theirs is the kingdom of heaven." Mathew 5: 10-12 NIV

Our journey with God will be full of persecution, the Bible is full of persecution, there is no avoiding it, it is one of Satan's weapons, a way to stop our journey with God. To make us want to go a different way, when we can bare it no longer, he wants us to turn away, give up, go back to our old ways, the persecution of Jesus was the ultimate evil, He was persecuted by His fellows Jews, by religious men.

We will not be hung on the cross but people will judge you, spread rumours about you, gossip about you, hate on you, falsely accuse you, and never be accountable for their own words and actions. They won't understand the change in you and if they won't like it, unless they too give themselves to Jesus.

People you consider friends may distance themselves from you, or you may want distance from them, as your life changes and you only want to please God. Satan will be trying to encourage others to be against you, through jealously and hate, or anything he can use against you.

Although the horse world is not as extreme as what Satan will try and put you though, there are definitely times where you are persecuted for no good reason, other than someone is jealous or doesn't like you. You learn to not be upset by what people say, by what people think or by people talking about you.

You learn to stay true to yourself, people rarely have the full story. They judge on what they see in front of them, not knowing how far the horse has come. They may say a horse lacks education for its age, without knowing the horse had previously been unrideable. Throwing many riders and trainers, over many years, and the fact the horse is now safe is a huge achievement, over the education level they feel you should have put on the horse.

Many people will blame you, or the horse, for their own lack of knowledge, they will falsely accuse you for the horse's actions, without wanting to understand how they themselves went wrong. They may say the horse doesn't know how to canter properly, when they themselves are bouncing around in the saddle, asking incorrectly, confusing the horse. Many would rather talk badly of you, rather than change themselves.

This lesson has very much come in handy along my God journey, especially when I have been unwell. I have no doubt many thought I left the horse industry due to my own failure, that I wasn't good enough, happy to talk badly about me, as they didn't and don't know my story. They don't know how ill I became, nor how much my life has changed in my journey with God. But the Bible says do not defend yourself, leave it to God, so be it. I don't know what the future holds, but I do know I definitely don't care what people say! God has only made me stronger in this conviction.

THANK YOU GOD

God used horses to teach me so many lessons over the years, I am now applying these to my relationship with Him. I do not doubt God blessed me with this opportunity to train horses. I pray that I am now walking the narrow path of the Lord, to the best of my abilities. I pray I am where God wants me to be. I pray I am making Him proud. I pray that I will continue to hear His guidance. I pray that I will continue to gain more wisdom. I pray I will forever get to know Him better. To do good. To love. For my only fear to ever be disappointing Him. Thank you God, for all your blessings and mercy, thank you Jesus for my salvation and thank you Holy Spirit for being my friend and helping me write every word of this testimony. All glory and honour are yours oh mighty Father. Amen.

Chapter 12

A WHOLE NEW PERSON

A whole new person in me has been born, as I continue to become more like Jesus, and ride the God roller-coaster! My testimony will be never ending, and unlike Jesus, us humans will make mistakes, but we must not forget we are saved, we must not lose faith, we must repent, stay turned towards God, everything is worth it.

DELIVERANCE:

Since first being delivered from depression, my mind is now free from so many oppressions. God allowing me to break many of these yokes off myself, has been a mind-blowing blessing, coming from childlike faith. Others were broken off me watching deliverance online, or through God using people like Josie. Although Satan tries constantly to trip me up, and have me open a door or allow a foothold, which does happen, but blessedly the oppressions broken to date have included:

Depression: I believed for years this was a part of my physical being, a very nasty voice in our heads.

Shame: along with guilt, was spoken over me since a child, I made others' lives harder, "why was I being like this", this is not from God.

Guilt: this has to go, to be released from the past, we are not that person anymore, guilt turns us away from God, eats away at us.

Leviathan: Pride! This will stop us ever getting full deliverance, stop us from being humble, very destructive in our lives, opens doors for so many emotions. Like a snake it strangles our progress.

Anxiety: like depression I thought this was something I had to manage forever. Incorrect. It causes our minds to run away from us. Makes small things seem huge.

Death: yeah, not happening!

Fear: like anxiety, such a revelation to be free, and one of Satan's favourites! It grips our minds like a vice.

Malice: ties in with unforgiveness, God forgave us, we must forgive, otherwise it will eat us up inside. Wanting someone to suffer because they hurt you is not of God.

Anger: another one of Satan favourites, he like to wind us up, poke the bear. This one of the easiest sins to slip back into, an evil merry go round, repent and get off! No matter how many times it takes.

Judgement: another sin that we commit without realising and needs constant repentance, why we must edit our thoughts.

Rebellion: teenagers are not the only rebellious one.

Taurus: we claim this when we read our horoscopes, ooops

Witchcraft: so easy to slip into new age beliefs these days, but creates a huge open door, a trap, which steals our peace and joy.

Jezebel: I'm still not sure if I had this one, but didn't want to risk pride or disbelief, to allow an open door. So I repented and evicted for good measure! It's the spirit that wants to control everything.

Disbelief: blocks wisdom, deliverance and healing.

Infirmity: I need to believe strongly this has been achieved, this yoke broken. Especially when I can see the psoriasis still on my skin. This may be a strong man in my life.

Pain: hard to distinguish where spiritual and physical lines are drawn.

Bitterness: this has been a really hard one, Satan tries to lure me back to anger a lot through bitterness, which gives him an open door to attack, he tries to drag my mind back to the past, especially where I have been treated unfairly, so I am constantly having to keep guard, throw off these thoughts. When I fail, do get angry and bitterness creeps in, I repent, constantly where needed. None of this is easy, but over time you get stronger and more practiced.

Curses: generational curses would no doubt exist over me, as we don't know all our families' pasts, or mistakes they made, agreements come into. Curses need to be dealt with to be free.

Devourer: destroys the blessings God has planned for us, steals the fruit of the spirit, the insects such as cankerworm, very important to rebuke.

Familiar spirits: I see these in dreams, pretending to be people I know, and am familiar with, but instead are trying to trick me, and keep track of me, so evil can attack at the moment of vulnerability.

Unworthiness: evil wants us to think we deserve no blessings, to drag ourselves into depression, pick ourselves apart, hate ourselves.

Soul ties: occur in many ways, particularly sex, it's why we should not have sex before marriage. We end up oppressed and depressed, we must break these yokes.

Rejection: a horrible feeling.

Confusion: speaks for itself, blocks the understanding the Holy Spirit provides, keeps us in bondage.

Marine spirit: will literally drag us under make us feel like we are drowning in anger, violence and madness.

Monitoring spirit: do exactly that, monitor us, collecting information that evil can use against us. Waiting to oppress us or trigger us, allowing marine spirits a door, we are then provoked to things like anger or judgement or bitterness.

Lieing spirit: we hear one thing but think we have heard another, twists our thoughts and others words.

Conniving spirit: plots and plans to trick us into sinning.

Lack: this is where the spiritual and physical cross over can be very much seen, lack of abundance that God has promised, can be financial, family, love, peace, joy.

Backward spirit: wants us to be Lots wife, miss out on the blessings we have due and are waiting for us.

Tormenting spirit: we must not let our minds beat ourselves up.

Slavery: makes us a slave to the flesh, things like money, beauty, winning become too important.

Python spirit: this is never submissive to God and causes much anguish as leads us away from the narrow path, where submission to God leads us to peace and joy. God plan for us is better than anything we could ever think up.

Orphan spirit: disconnection and insecurity and uncertainty. None of these emotions are pleasant, we can be free of them.

Addiction: this can encompass many things, for me cigarettes was a big one.

Envy: so easy to look at others and wish we had what they have, it allows torment in.

Unforgiveness: one of the worst sins. it leaves a huge open door for all the spirits to come attack you. There is no excuse, we must forgive to move forward in the kingdom.

STRONG MAN: this is the head man, the leader of the legion, he rules over all the demons within you. Breaking his hold breaks the hold of the other spirits as well, but takes someone being granted much authority by God. It took 5 days of fasting and prayer to break his hold over me, but thank God I now feel much freer and much more at peace, more self-aware, and it's much harder for anger and bitterness to be triggered in me.

Emotions that I was struggling to be free from. Satan kept throwing up challenges in the physical to keep me trapped.

STRONG HOLDS: this is where demos hide, rather than being delivered it is a process over time to break them, it requires renewal of the mind to break them down, piece by piece they are dismantled, as we grow stronger in the Lord, more like Jesus.

As my journey has progressed there has been so very many spirits, I've needed deliverance from, and it doesn't end here. It takes digging deep and letting the Holy Spirit educate you to even admit to yourself that these spirits exist within you. Whether it be from your own sin or words, or from those of generations past, abuse, or others word cursing you or having ill intent, there are so many ways evil uses to oppress us, to attach itself to us.

Living without these evils, depression and anxiety especially, is a total revelation in itself, such a huge burden lifted. Life is so very much easier, the peace and joy from God is the most wonderful way to live.

Having renounced and been delivered from these oppressions does not mean I walk around in peace and joy all the time, but percentage wise there has been a dramatic increase. Whereas before I would maybe have 1 good day a week, now I have many days and weeks where I feel totally content in the love of Jesus, total faith in God's plan for me moving forward. Other days I get tripped up, worry creeps in the flesh gets loud. I try to figure out how the future will work, whether it be financially, my health or my children, but in reality, I shouldn't do this, I should have my full faith in God, capture and evict those lines of thought. Trust that he has a plan I know nothing about, which will be revealed in His time. This narrow path is not easy, I am after all still flesh, and a very new Christian with still much to learn.

But most of the time, the God sized hole in my heart is full to over flowing. I have become much more adept at editing my thoughts before they run away from me, and I start to believe Satan lies. I am in much less torment, my armour is much more easily worn and understood, especially the sword, His word. Learning how to wield this and pray with scripture, has very much helped me keep Satan at bay. Especially in my dreams. Psalm 91 is a daily prayer I declare over my life. Holy Spirit has used Psalm 91 for me to understand the next level of declaring over my life, how to wield the word. How safe and protected I am dwelling in God in all areas of my life.

I now also understand that when these bad days come, that Satan is trying hardest to push me from the narrow path. That trials are required to move forward, that in fact it's because he knows that just around the next corner, is a blessing he doesn't want me to have, a blessing that will further defeat his kingdom. I must resist his lies, know that God is refining me for bigger things to come and that Satan can in fact only attack with Gods permission, or because I've allowed access through legal rights. It is just up to me to keep the faith, not to worry, and that soon will come a God moment, that will lift me up with joy and understanding. Fill me up with the love of Jesus, a Holy Spirit hug, another step forward on the narrow path.

CANCER:

My blessings have continued, but the trials don't end.

Surgery: I finally got a date right near Halloween, the hospital called telling me, "The surgery is scheduled for next week, but because the public system is full, we are going to put you in a private hospital instead!"

Praise God.

Then once I was in hospital, just like I had claimed and declared, the surgery was successful, no complications, no pain, and just so I knew it was an act of God. I woke up in a private room, with a window, which gave me a good chuckle as that was Josie's declaration and testimony not mine! God absolutely has a sense of humour! All glory too Him.

But in saying that, too many blessings Satan hates, so he came in under the radar. I got a staph infection in the wound 2 weeks later, right after I had been praying Psalm 91 over Merroo! But although my doctor was concerned, I may need to be admitted to hospital for I.V. antibiotics, everyone prayed over me, and declared that would not be the case. Done says God, and flicks away Satan attempts, no I.V. needed.

Then came the waiting for the final results, the tests done on the part of my thyroid which had been removed. The decider of the future, if more surgery and treatment was needed. I off course fought this with continued faith and declaration. I declared every cancer cell had been removed, I declared no more surgery would be needed, I declared I would not need thyroid drug's, I declared no further treatment would be needed. God had brought me this far, no way I wasn't going to believe for a full home run.

I was due to return to the specialist offices 4 weeks after surgery, it was a Tuesday in early December, as I sat there waiting, I heard the reception calling people telling them the surgeon was running late. Very unusual, so expected to be waiting at least an hour. I prayed and declared in my head, the clock ticked, then the receptionist made an announcement to all of us waiting. The surgeon had fallen ill, he was off to the hospital himself. She would call to reschedule, dang well played Satan, wasn't expecting that! I would need to keep praying.

She called later that day. Saturday 9.40pm.

I arrived Saturday all prayed up, better than that actually, as I was due to be baptised the following day, I had been fasting since Wednesday. I wanted as much spiritual strength as possible, but the night before I had had a dream. A warning from God or an attack I don't know, in the dream familiar spirits in the form of my brother and his ex-partner had come to tell me they had cancer, much worse than my own. I cancelled and rebuked it, not understanding.

Sitting again in the waiting room, the surgeon came and got my file, then was gone awhile before calling me in. He had a look on his face I didn't like, I was so confident for getting the results I had been declaring, too confident maybe, maybe I wasn't humble enough. Maybe God just has other plans.

But the results were closer to the dream, 3rd times a charm for evil to attack, the results told me that although the original cancer that had been detected was smaller than first thought at only 3mm, a miracle that it had even been biopsied successfully to start. Because I count every blessing. But strangely it had spread to my lymph nodes, of the 15 removed 5 had cancer, not good. I would now need further surgery to remove the other half of my thyroid, followed by radioactive iodine treatment. Both requiring stays in hospital, the surgery was booked for March, followed a couple months later by the RAI. Then medication every day for the rest of my life to replace the lack of thyroid.

This was exactly the results I didn't want. I wobbled emotionally; the worry started to creep in. But then I realised, Satan is a liar! My declarations are still correct. Every cancer cell has been removed from my body! The mass in my thyroid and offending lymph nodes are out of my body.

The next surgery and RAI are to make sure of this, a precaution. But I actually haven't had any further treatments yet! Nor have I started medication! This comes into line with my declarations!

Which means, there is still time for every declaration to be truth! God can still do things we can't even comprehend. I just have to keep declaring that I won't need further treatment, I won't need medication, it's not up to me to use my human brain and figure out how this will come to pass. I just have to have faith and believe it will.

I need to see it as a test, a refining, a stretching, something that will make me stronger. It hasn't pushed me off the narrow path. I have lost zero faith in God, if that's Satan intent then he has 100% failed, I also have zero fear or worry, my life is not at risk.

If anything, I know that God has plans to make my testimony even bigger and better, more useful to others, by having this test when I do get more miracles there can be no doubt in anyone's mind about my healing, God's blessing, my faith. They can't say it was just a mistake from the beginning, that I got lucky, when God acts, I'll have 100% proof of a miracle. My journey will also show others that it was never just an easy path, that I got tested and was pushed to lose hope, to lose faith, but I didn't not for one second. I also never lost my peace or joy, that it is possible, that God is always there for us. That we need to wear our armour provided, that we can kick Satan's butt every day of the week, no matter how much he tries to attack and trick us! Praise Jesus bring it on! My spirit man grows stronger every day in the refining fire.

AUTO IMMUNE DISEASES:

My physical health has been one of Satan's greatest targets, with my immune system also under attack, to the point it is destroying my own body. I have chosen not to write about this in too much detail, as words have so much power, I've chosen not to accept the doctor's words or treatments. I rebuke these auto immune issues, and will continue to have expectations of healing. Claiming Gods word and promises. I have faith, but perhaps there are demons I have yet to discover that need evicting for this to happen, or unforgiveness in my heart. That wisdom, I don't doubt, is just around the next corner, I will continue to strengthen my spirit man, pray and sharpen my sword of His word, so when God timing is right this is a fight I will win, and come into full health which has eluded me for so long, and then I can add it to my testimony, give the Lord all the glory that His mercy and grace provides, praise Jesus.

HORSES:

One of the final parts of my current testimony, is probably the part that has been one of the most unexpected. The title of this book and a huge part of my journey, was how God used all that I have learnt about myself through my relationship with horses, to develop my relationship with Him, but now I find myself completely losing interest in the horses and that side of my life.

Horses consumed so much of my mind, and my time for so long. They were my passion, my sanity, my joy, my life.

God has now taken all those places, God is now my passion, my sanity, my joy, my life. I'm 1000 times happier now, than I ever was before. I have no clue what the future holds. If God will place me back using those talents again, but in a less consuming way. Many relationships I valued have become distant, as those people are not on the same God journey I am. We are just at different places in our lives, but God has not left me on this journey alone, many women I was previously only acquainted with, have now become close friends. Along with a whole new group of amazing women through Merroo, whom I learn so much from, and who go to war with me when needed.

I know God is taking me to a new place, a new season, better than I have ever known before, even without the horses the future is bright, a new thing has begun, the supernatural is bringing everything into alignment. It is very exciting the God roller-coaster, I must never be Lots wife and look backwards only forwards, to follow the narrow path with my gazed fixed solidly on God, is where peace and joy is found like I have never experienced before. The Lord's purpose will prevail, thank you, thank you Jesus all glory and honour is yours. Amen.

I will close my current testimony with an event:

> On the 10th of December 2023, approximately 2 years after hearing the voice of God, approximately 2years from the day my whole life changed forever. 2 years since I met my greatest loves, God, Jesus and the Holy Spirit. I was baptised at Merroo, what an amazing day with my amazing new Merroo family, I appreciate them all so very much, the future is bright and amazing. Thankyou Jesus. I'm excited and expectant for the amazing journey ahead, show me the way Lord. I "know" the journey will be great. Amen.

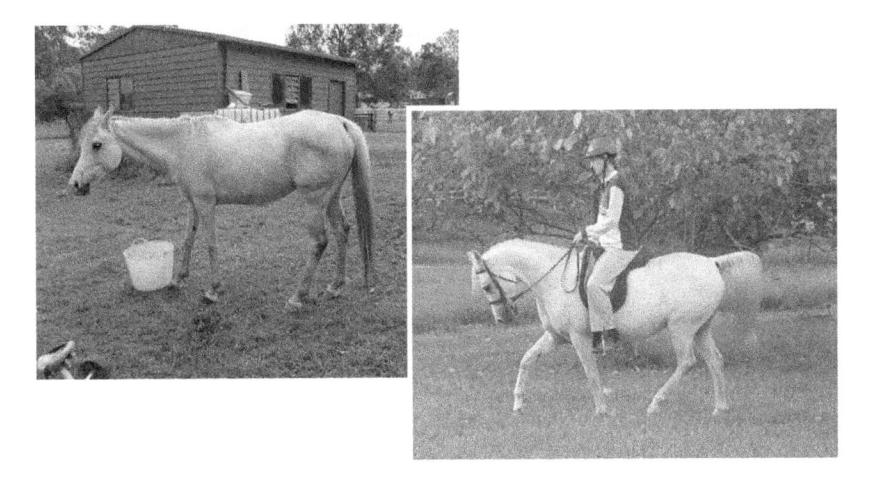

Above: Before and after photos of the horse that started my journey to becoming a professional.

Below: Floods are an intense but beautiful force of nature. The first photo was taken by a neighbour, but as you can see by the chicken house structure, the water rose much higher.

Above: For over 10 years horses were my whole life.

Below left: A photo taken after thyroid surgery, feeling like God was looking out for me.
Below right: Baptism Day, with Josie and Pastor David, at Merroo.